T0323595

Cambridge Elements ≡

Elements in Historical Theory and Practice
edited by
Daniel Woolf
Queen's University, Ontario

HISTORIANS' AUTOBIOGRAPHIES AS HISTORIOGRAPHICAL INQUIRY

A Global Perspective

Jaume Aurell
University of Navarra

CAMBRIDGE
UNIVERSITY PRESS

Shaftesbury Road, Cambridge CB2 8EA, United Kingdom

One Liberty Plaza, 20th Floor, New York, NY 10006, USA

477 Williamstown Road, Port Melbourne, VIC 3207, Australia

314–321, 3rd Floor, Plot 3, Splendor Forum, Jasola District Centre,
New Delhi – 110025, India

103 Penang Road, #05–06/07, Visioncrest Commercial, Singapore 238467

Cambridge University Press is part of Cambridge University Press & Assessment,
a department of the University of Cambridge.

We share the University's mission to contribute to society through the pursuit of
education, learning and research at the highest international levels of excellence.

www.cambridge.org
Information on this title: www.cambridge.org/9781009539418

DOI: 10.1017/9781009396912

First published 2024

A catalogue record for this publication is available from the British Library

ISBN 978-1-009-53941-8 Hardback
ISBN 978-1-009-39690-5 Paperback
ISSN 2634-8616 (online)
ISSN 2634-8608 (print)

Cambridge University Press & Assessment has no responsibility for the persistence
or accuracy of URLs for external or third-party internet websites referred to in this
publication and does not guarantee that any content on such websites is, or will
remain, accurate or appropriate.

Historians' Autobiographies as Historiographical Inquiry

A Global Perspective

Elements in Historical Theory and Practice

DOI: 10.1017/9781009396912
First published online: December 2024

Jaume Aurell
University of Navarra

Author for correspondence: Jaume Aurell, saurell@unav.es

Abstract: This Element analyses the autobiographies of historians from a global perspective and looks at all eras, from antiquity to the present day. It includes twenty autobiographies: Caesar's and Lucian of Samosata's memories in antiquity; an autobiography of a medieval king such as Peter IV of Aragon; Vico's, Gibbon's and Adams' intellectual self-accounting in modernity; autobiographical revelations and social activism of twentieth century women historians such as Carolyn Steedman, Jill Conway and Gerda Lerner; classical Chinese and Islamic traditions through the autobiographies of Sima Quian and Ibn Khaldun; the perplexities inherent in the modernisation of Japan (Fukuzawa Yukichi), China (Gu Jiegang), India (Nirad Chaudhuri) and Egypt (Taha Hussein); postmodernists such as Rosenstone; and traumatic postcolonial experiences in Africa (Bethwell Ogot), Latin America (Carlos Eire) and Southeast Asia (Wang Gungwu). This Element proposes a literary and historical approach to these autobiographies, emphasising its historiographical dimension and value.

Keywords: historiography, autobiography, gender, postcolonial, biography

ISBNs: 9781009539418 (HB), 9781009396905 (PB), 9781009396912 (OC)
ISSNs: 2634-8616 (online), 2634-8608 (print)

Contents

Introduction

This project has its origins in Daniel Woolf's invitation to write a book on the autobiographies of historians, for inclusion in the Cambridge University Press series 'Elements in Historical Theory and Practice'. Daniel knew I had already written a monograph on the subject, *Theoretical Perspectives on Historians' Autobiographies* (2016), confined to twentieth-century Western historians. He suggested that I write a book with a global scope, from Japan to Latin America, and a long-term perspective, from antiquity to the present day. That was a real but stimulating challenge.

I began by asking myself how I became interested in this peculiar historical-literary genre. Serendipity, a circumstance so common in our research, led me to Robert A. Rosenstone's article 'Confessions of a Postmodern (?) Historian' (2004), a short autobiographical essay full of rhetorical paradoxes and theoretical turns.[1] The author took an ironic and sceptical approach to his intellectual journey. I was fascinated by the possibility of recreating one's own academic itinerary without letting go of one's own identity as a citizen, intellectual, scholar and historian – or, more precisely, by *using* all those categories.

A colleague subsequently advised me to read Georges Duby's *History Continues* (1991).[2] Duby describes the main steps of a historian's career – from their early studies to preparing their dissertation, embarking on their teaching career, entering the public arena and eventually their more mature historiographical production. I realised then the exemplary potential of this genre, and decided to recommend it to my doctoral students. In addition, I soon realised that Duby's academic memoir was part of a larger movement of French historians, coordinated by Pierre Nora and labelled *ego-histoire*.[3]

I continued to read, at first occasionally and then compulsively, other autobiographies of historians. I was reminded of the Socratic maxim proclaimed by Plato: 'the unexamined life is not worth living'. The critical bibliography on autobiography (Philippe Lejeune, Karl J. Weintraub, Paul J. Eakin, Jeremy Popkin, Melanie Nolan) and the new theories of the narrative nature of the historical operation (Lionel Gossman, Philippe Carrard, Leo Braudy, Peter Gay, John Clive, Jack Hexter, Ann Rigney, Hayden White) kept me thinking about the whole subgenre of historians' autobiographies. Both as an intellectual and a citizen, the historian has a special social and public responsibility, and must therefore scrutinise not only the quality of their work but also the whole ethical dimension surrounding it.

---

[1] Robert A. Rosenstone, 'Confessions of a Postmodern (?) Historian', *Rethinking History* 8 (2004): 149–166.

[2] Georges Duby, *History Continues* (Chicago: The University of Chicago Press, 1994).

[3] Pierre Nora, ed., *Essais d'ego-histoire* (Paris: Gallimard, 1987).

It was not just about my personal and intellectual enrichment from these readings. My own training as a historian was also at stake since, as E. H. Carr stated in his classic *What Is History?*, 'I shall venture to believe that the historian who is most conscious of his own situation is also most capable of transcending it'[4] – transcending their own context is what historians who decide to write their autobiography do. According to this, Carr himself chose as the basic idea of his book the sentence: 'Study the historian before you begin to study the facts.'[5] Paul Valéry expressed the same idea, though perhaps with more poetry and sophistication: 'there is no theory that is not in fact a carefully concealed part of the theorist's own life story'.[6] Gabrielle M. Spiegel pursued the same idea from a more specifically academic and historiographical perspective: 'It is my profound conviction that what we do as historians is to write, in highly displaced, usually unconscious, but nonetheless determined ways, our inner, personal obsessions.'[7]

The qualified testimonies of Carr, Valéry and Spiegel confirm that the life of the historian is inseparable from their work and relevant for the theories that feed it. The historical operation is a continuous exercise in realism, in which the ability to observe exterior reality as well as interior conscience has to proceed simultaneously – the retrospective with the introspective. The perception of one's own consciousness and subjectivity, and a critical approach to them, is an indispensable condition for being able to discern and objectify the past. Readings of historians' autobiographies thus become a platform for understanding the dynamics of historical work itself, while at the same time providing us with indispensable epistemic and ethical tools for its practice.

Almost unconsciously, my compulsive reading of historians' autobiographies led me to regard this subgenre not only as an opportunity to improve my training as a historian, but also as a specific *historiographical* genre that deserved to be systematically analysed in the same way as I had done with my own medieval historical subjects such as Mediterranean merchant culture, Catalan chronicles, and European self-coronations. When I began to consider and work on this possibility, I could not have imagined that the number of historians' autobiographies would be so large that it would be necessary to restrict the chronology and regions analysed. I eventually decided to focus on autobiographies by twentieth-century Western historians, mainly European,

---

[4] Edward H. Carr, *What Is History?* (London: Penguin, 1987), 53.
[5] Carr, *What Is History?*, 23.
[6] Quoted in Jerome Klinkowitz, *Rosenberg, Barthes, Hassan: The Postmodern Habit of Thought* (Athens: University of Georgia Press, 1988), 118.
[7] Gabrielle M. Spiegel, 'France for Belgium' in *Why France? American Historians Reflect on an Enduring Fascination*, eds. Laura Lee Downs and Stéphane Gerson (Ithaca: Cornell University Press, 2007), 89.

American and Australian. I thought that, with such a restricted approach, the corpus of my literary-historical research would be considerably reduced. It proved to be a naïve assumption, since the number of autobiographies to be considered kept growing until it reached 500.

Yet I realised that these literary-historiographical artefacts were original and relevant. Their originality and, therefore, their charm lie in the ability of certain historians to proceed retrospectively when carrying out an introspective analysis of their own lives. They have a particular talent for connecting the general context that has governed their lives with their personal itinerary, which only they can reveal. They are at the crucial crossroads between the subjective and the objective, the private and the public, the retrospective and the introspective, the intimate and the unveiled. These are spheres from which historians cannot disengage, and so the historians' autobiographies become not only literary artefacts, but also a relevant source of intellectual history (as diaries, correspondence and other personal documents) and an intellectual event in themselves.

* * *

With these assumptions in mind, this Element aims to highlight the literary, historical and historiographical value of historians' autobiographies. I argue that history university curricula should include some of these historians' autobiographies, or even offer new courses focusing on them. In fact, the selection criteria for the twenty autobiographies presented as case studies in this volume, from the Chinese Sima Qian to the multicultural Wang Gungwu, and from the classic Caesar to the postcolonial African Bethwell Ogot, are governed by their paradigmatic character, their global scope and their educative potential.

The Element's long-term chronological scope and global span show that historians in all eras have used the autobiographical genre for different purposes, from Caesar's political memoirs in antiquity and Vico's and Gibbon's intellectual self-accounting in early modernity to the more recent autobiographical revelations and social activism of Gerda Lerner and Carlos Eire. The Element's global scope allows us to enter the classical Chinese and Islamic traditions through the autobiographies of Sima Qian and Ibn Khaldun, the perplexities inherent in the modernisation of Japan (Fukuzawa Yukichi), China (Gu Jiegang), India (Nirad Chaudhuri) and Egypt (Taha Hussein), as well as the traumatic experiences arising from postcolonisation processes in Africa (Bethwell Ogot), Latin America (Carlos Eire) and Southeast Asia (Wang Gungwu).

When these authoritative historians write about their *own* pasts, their writings become a relevant tool for the study not only of their particular lives and contexts, but also of the practice of history. They become sources of cultural and intellectual history, and (some of them) valuable literary narrations. Villehardouin's *Memoir of Crusade*, for example, was an authentic bestseller in his time; Vico's narration of his own life serves the objective of consciousness of what is true in the coherence of what is done and what is reasoned; Gibbon's *Memoirs of My Life* embodies the Enlightenment figure of the historian-philosopher, and the quality of his personal narrative secured his place in the pantheon of classics of the autobiographical genre. *The Education of Henry Adams* has consistently appeared on the list of the most influential nonfiction books of the twentieth century and had an enormous impact on the American culture and education of its time. Carolyn Steedman's, Jill Ker Conway's and Gerda Lerner's autobiographies are written at a gallop, read like gripping novels, and have been acclaimed as compelling testimonies to women's struggle for equality, not only influential intellectual accounts but also literary writing of high quality. Carlos Eire's childhood autobiography received the US National Book Award for Nonfiction in 2003, was hailed as an exceptional book, has been translated into multiple languages and sold close to half a million copies, which speak volumes for the potential of historians' autobiographies. Robert A. Rosenstone's two autobiographies are revealing testimonies to what postmodern irony and imagination can bring to historiography. All of them – and the others included in this Element – use their own life stories as an element of historiographical understanding, disciplinary intervention and personal involvement in social agendas and activism.

Apart from their inherent historical and historiographical interest, I also intend this Element to help give historians' autobiographies a greater presence in the fields of literature and literary criticism. They are certainly historical artefacts because the historicist mentality of their authors conditions their content. But they also have literary value, since some of them – I am thinking especially of Gibbon, Adams, Chaudhuri, Hussein, Steedman, Conway, Lerner, Rosenstone and Eire – are stories in which imagination plays an essential role and the narrative is wonderfully well-spun.

Considering that, as Hayden White has argued, all historical artefacts are composed of content – the part of the narrative in the present that seeks an analogy with the past – *and* form – the narrative itself – I also propose in this Element to trace the long-term transformations of the genre of historians' autobiographies. From the unconventional forms of the autobiographies of antiquity – that is, Sima Qian's epistolary genre, Caesar's panegyrical self-eulogy and Lucian's referential dream – to the more recent properly literary autobiographies by Jill Ker Conway, Gerda Lerner or Carlos Eire, this genre has undergone radical transformations that are worth highlighting. They also reflect to a large extent the evolution of autobiography generically considered, from the spiritual autobiographies of antiquity and early modernity, such as Augustine's,

Abelard's, and Theresa's, to the intimate autobiographies of modernity by Jean-Jacob Rousseau and Gabriel García Márquez.

* * *

This Element follows a chronological approach in six sections. Each of them critically approaches the autobiographies that seem to me to be most representative, and is completed with general comments on the evolution of the genre in the respective period.

The first section is devoted to the autobiography of historians in antiquity. In this period, we can speak neither of a body of professional historians nor of an autobiographical genre as such, but we have preserved some first-person narratives written by authors who have dealt with the past in their works. The selected texts are the *Letter to Ren An* by the classical Chinese historian Sima Qian (c. 96 BC), the *Gallic War* and the *Civil War* first-person narratives by Caesar (c. 58–49 BC), and the autobiographical *Dream* by the Greek-speaking and Syrian-Roman writer Lucian of Samosata (c. 165). Classical antiquity functions, once again, as an archetype of successive autobiographical forms, since these three texts prefigure academic works such as modern political memoirs such as Winston Churchill's *Memoirs* (1948–1953), Eric Hobsbawm's *Interesting Times* (2002) and imaginative ventures such as Carlos Eire's *Waiting for Snow in Havana* (2003).

The second section deals with autobiography in the Middle Ages. The genre reaches literary maturity, although it entails specific proposals such as an ideological claim (Geoffrey of Villehardouin's *Memoirs of Crusade*, c. 1213), political legitimisation (King Peter the Ceremonious' *Llibre*, 1375) or civilisational exploration (Ibn Khaldun's *Travel Memoirs*, 1405). These demonstrate the predisposition that the medieval audience had for first-person historical narratives, whose legitimacy came from the authority of the direct testimony of their authors rather than the external referentiality demanded by modern audiences.

In Western modernity, which is the subject of the third section, historian-autobiographers tend to focus on cognitive and educational questions and establish the model of the modern *bildungsroman*, as is the case with Vico's *Autobiography* (1731), Gibbon's *Memoirs of My Life* (1795) and *The Education of Henry Adams* (1907). These texts also reflect the successive phases of modernisation in the West, from the original rationalism of Vico to the British Enlightenment of Gibbon and the liberal American paroxysm of Adams.

The fourth section concerns Japanese, Chinese, Hindu and Islamic colonial testimonies from the first half of the twentieth century. They evidence perplexity at the deep problems associated with the processes of modernisation, industrialisation, rationalisation and westernisation as dramatically experienced by these different civilisations, moving between idealisation and repulsion, in Meiji Japan

(Fukuzawa's *Autobiography*, 1899), Marxist China (Gu Jiegang's *Autobiography*, 1931), British India (Chaudhuri's *Autobiography of Unknown India*, 1951) and Islamic Egypt (Taha Hussein's *The Days*, 1967). Beyond their strict historiographical interest, these texts are dramatic testimonies of the tectonic clash that took place from the mid nineteenth century between centuries-old traditions and the galloping modernisation – or should we say 'westernisation'? – generated by colonialism.

In the middle of the twentieth century, the authorial voice of women emerged with great force as they entered university studies and teaching. The autobiographies of women historians – the content of the fifth section – are a particularly eloquent manifestation of this relevant intellectual, literary and scholarly activity. When they practice autobiography women historians embark on a literary journey that not only informs historically but also ponders morally and delves into life's most transcendent questions. The enjoyable self-reports of Carolyn Steedman (*Landscape for a Good Woman*, 1986), Jill K. Conway (*True North*, 1994) and Gerda Lerner (*Fireweed*, 2003) lead us to continually question the morality and exemplarity of our own lives. They are a testament to how a historian's autobiography can become an exciting literary narrative without losing its historicity.

Finally, in the sixth section, the most recent historians with a postcolonial and postmodern sensibility, namely the African Bethwell Allan Ogot (*My Footprints on the Sands of Time*, 2003), the Cuban-American Carlos Eire (*Waiting for Snow in Havana*, 2003), the Canadian-American Robert A. Rosenstone (*Adventures of a Postmodern Historian*, 2016) and the Asian/Australasian Wang Gungwu (*Home Is Where We Are*, 2018), provide the global, inter-civilisational and inter-ethnic vision necessary today to understand the world and its cultural dynamics.

1 Ancient Politics

Sima Qian, Caesar, Lucian of Samosata

It is difficult to speak of autobiography as such in the ancient world. Critics agree that the first autobiographical book written with the intention of being disseminated is the *Confessions* of Augustine of Hippo, written in late antiquity around 398. At the same time, there was no professional historiography as we know it today. Therefore, the subjects selected for this section are writers interested in the analysis of the past who have left some *stories* about themselves rather than properly engaging in providing an integrated account of their own lives: the *Letter to Ren An* by Sima Qian (c. 96 BC), the *Gallic War* and the *Civil War* first-person narratives by Caesar (c. 58–49 BC), and the autobiographical *Dream* by the Greek-speaking Syrian-Roman writer Lucian of Samosata (c. 165).

Each of these texts represents an archetypal reality, which will be replicated by successive generations of autobiographical historians. Sima uses his letter to express his frustration over some of the injustices that have led him to inner prostration and public marginalisation. His legitimising intention in claiming for an elusive justice will be replicated by other autobiographies described in later sections such as those by Ibn Khaldun, Fukuzawa, Gu, Chaudhuri, Hussein, Lerner and Ogot.

In other authors, autobiography acquires a vindictive component with political implications which are taken up, almost verbatim, from Caesar's war memoirs. The rhetorical line running from Caesar's journals to Winston Churchill's Second World War memoirs is easy to follow. Churchill describes the spirit of these accounts: 'I have followed the method of Defoe's *Memoirs of a Cavalier*, in which the author hangs the chronicle and discussion of great military and political events upon the thread of the personal experiences of an individual.'[8] Most of the autobiographies included in this Element are authored by intellectuals, but the political memoirs of the likes of Caesar and Churchill testify to the relevance and influence of the subgenre of political autobiography since antiquity. The memoirs of King Peter of Aragon, a ruler with an extraordinary historical sensitivity, are another clear manifestation of this trend, included in the section on the Middle Ages.

Finally, Lucian of Samosata's memoir, presented in the form of a dream, inaugurates the imaginative line of historians' autobiographies, which will be taken up again in the Middle Ages, especially in *El Somni* ('The Dream', 1399) by the Catalan ruler Bernat Metge, who used this subgenre to legitimise his political action in the face of corruption charges. Modernity is not comfortable with this autobiographical tendency to dreams and imagination, as the hyper-rationalist autobiographers in Section 3 – Vico, Gibbon, Adams – confirm. But the tradition will be taken up by some postmodern historians, such as Robert A. Rosenstone in his *Adventures of a Postmodern Historian* (2016) and Carlos Eire with *Waiting for Snow in Havana* (2003), discussed in the last section.

The examples gathered in this section show that all autobiographies can be read either at the level of event or of representation. If Sima's autobiography is a model of *historiographical* meaning – the representations of the events – Caesar's memoirs have *historical* validity in themselves. The former speaks about the historical operation and its dynamics, while the latter functions as a primary source. If Sima's autobiography tells us a lot about the determined will of historians to get on with their work, Caesar's autobiography is a valid

---

[8] Quoted in Richard Cohen, *Making History: The Storytellers Who Shaped the Past* (London: Weidenfeld & Nicolson, 2022), 435.

testimony to the heuristic dimension of this genre. Sima tells us about of his feelings about the historical work as its author, while the Roman autocrat functions as a memoirist who writes a history of events in which he has played a significant part.

This leads us to our first relevant distinction within the genre of historians' autobiographies. When an autobiography is written by an intellectual who is predominantly engaged in history – what, from Ranke onwards, we will call 'a professional historian' – the genre sheds considerable light on the dynamics of the historical operation itself. When an autobiography is written by someone with the capacity to 'make history' in the broad sense of the term as recently used by Richard Cohen, where the author is not necessarily a professional historian but a character with a historical sensibility such as Clarendon, Voltaire, Ulysses S. Grant or Churchill, then the genre itself functions as a historical rather than a historiographical artefact. Characters like Caesar and Churchill 'make history' in a double sense: both as relevant historical figures worthy of appearing in history books and as history makers with the histories they write.

Sima Qian's Autobiographical Letter (96 BC)

> *I would have despised myself for dying*
> *before the glory of my writings*
> *could be displayed to later generations.*[9]

These words reflect well the passion for history of Sima Qian (145–86 BC), considered the classic among classics: to keep writing history, he opted for the shame of living as a castrate rather than the glory of a heroic death.

Sima has rightly been labelled the father of Chinese historiography, just as Herodotus is the father of Western historiography. He worked tirelessly on his monumental *Records of the Grand Historian*, a history of the first twenty-four generations of China. This narrative covers more than 2,000 years of the History of China, beginning in the legendary age of Hunagdi, the Yellow Emperor, and ending in Sima's own time, with Emperor Wu of Han. This text has been considered as not only a classic work of history and model for history writing but also one of the foundations of Chinese civilisation. Most of the Chinese emblematic and mythologised figures such as Confucius or the first emperor of the Quin dynasty were modulated by Sima's historical narratives.

---

[9] Stephen Durrant, Wai-yee Li, Michael Nylan, Hans van Ess, eds., *The Letter to Ren An. Sima Qian's Legacy* (Seattle: University of Washington Press, 2016), 28. On Sima, see Esther Klein, *Reading Sima Qian from Han to Song: The Father of History in Pre-Modern China* (Leiden: Brill, 2018) and Grant Hardy, *Worlds of Bronze and Bamboo: Sima Qian's Conquest of History* (New York: Columbia University Press, 1999).

Sima was born in Longmen, under the rule of the Han dynasty. He was the son of Sima Tan, an official of the imperial government, and worked as a chief scribe at the Han court. Like Herodotus, he travelled to gather information for his work, visiting the imperial capital, Chang'an (near present-day Xi'an), the Yangtze River, the Kingdom of Changsha (Hunan Province), the cities of Shaoxing, Huaiyin (Jiangsu Province) and Qufu, the hometown of Confucius, where he studied rituals and other traditional subjects.

Around 99 BC, the knights Li Ling and Li Guangli fought the Xiongnu in northern China, where they were defeated and taken captive. Emperor Wu attributed their defeat to Li Ling's incompetence and cowardice. All government officials joined the emperor in his condemnation, except Sima. Although he had never been close friends with Li Ling, he respected him and felt it necessary to defend him from ignominy – *noblesse oblige*. The emperor interpreted Sima's defence as an attack on his brother-in-law, Li Guangli, who had also been defeated by the Xiongnu, and sentenced Sima to death. He could redeem the execution with money or castration. As Sima did not have enough money, he opted for castration and was imprisoned for three years. Defeated, isolated and having abandoned all hope, Sima wrote a letter to Ren An Shaoqing, another court official, to justify his position and explain why he had not committed suicide: considering castration to be the worst of all punishments, he said the only thing that kept him alive was his dedication to history.

What was a painful heart-rending plea of personal defence is for us a historical pearl, for through this autobiographical letter we can gain insight into the soul of this great historian and his context. When he was castrated, he had yet to complete his manuscript on the great history of China. So, he concludes, if only *that* history could be completed successfully, he would not have any regrets, even if he were to suffer ten thousand deaths.[10] Those of us dedicated to this fascinating activity realise that in history we have a vocation rather than a profession. However, it is difficult to find a parallel of Sima's determination, with perhaps the sole exception of Socrates and his attachment to philosophy. Sima's autobiographical letter also recalls another 'personal calamity' as suffered by the medieval intellectual Peter Abelard and recounted in is *History of My Calamities* (c. 1132), a sort of autobiography written in the literary form of a letter.

Sima's autobiographical letter can be read as a justification for an injustice – or, alternatively, as an original way of answering the following question: 'Why devote your life to writing history?' The autobiographies of historians always have an exemplary value, and here again Sima acts as the originator of a trend. The profession of historian is not something externally or artificially assimilated.

---

[10] Durrant, *The Letter to Ren An*, 29.

Rather, it is a reality embedded in one's own life, which channels and governs one's entire existence.

In his letter, Sima presents himself as the director of the court archives. He feels his body ruined and debased, and his spirit fallen and defeated. The effect of his castration has been devastating, both on his body and his soul. His body has been mutilated beyond repair and his soul has been lacerated by an unjust accusation. However, he has tried to cultivate, since childhood, the five virtues so dear to Chinese culture:

> I have heard that self-cultivation is the storehouse of wisdom; magnanimity, the beginning of humaneness; discernment, the mark of dutifulness; shame, after disgrace the decisive factor in courage; and the desire to leave a good name, the ultimate wellspring of good behaviour. Only after a gentleman possesses these five virtues can he be commended to his generation and listed in the ranks of the truly noble.[11]

None of his acquaintances came to his defence at that dramatic moment. His loneliness was particularly hurtful for Sima because 'a body is not made of wood or stone!'[12] All that remains for him is the possibility of leaving some trace through his historical writings. His wish is to narrate the past while thinking of future generations.

The dignity with which Sima bore his calamity, the determination with which he went on with his historical work and the sustaining awareness of his vocation as a historian are three qualities that comfort him in the hardest moments of his work. Without having to suffer what Sima suffered, we have all experienced, at times, the historical task becoming heavy, and the glory of results slow in coming. After his release from prison in 96 BC, he resumed his historical activity and served at the Han court as an archivist. This was a post reserved for eunuchs and, as it was a respected profession, he was able to regain some of its lost reputation and, most important for him, he could then complete his task and rest in pace.

To me, the *Letter to Ren An* is an eloquent testimony to the agony with which some of the all-time great historical narratives have been conceived under dramatic circumstances, such as Marc Bloch's *Strange Defeat* or Henri Pirenne's *Mahomet et Charlemagne*, elaborated in the middle of the horrors of war, and to the thousands of historians who are suffering persecution under authoritarian regimes. The first of the autobiographies analysed in this Element leaves us with this first teaching: that the historical task is so sublime that it is worth the effort to carry it out, even amidst the harshest hardships.

---

[11] Durrant, *The Letter to Ren An*, 29.   [12] Durrant, *The Letter to Ren An*, 26.

Caesar's War Memoirs (58–49 BC)

Gallia est omnis divisa in partes tres.[13]

Gaius Julius Caesar (100–44 BC) was the Roman general who led the Roman armies in the conquest of the Gallia between 58 and 51 BC and wrote his experiences in *Commentarii de bello Gallico* ('The Gallic War'). After this first victory, he defeated his new rival, Pompey, in a civil war, which was also narrated by Caesar in *Commentarii de Bello Civili* ('The Civil War'). He became dictator of the Roman Republic from 49 BC until his assassination in 44 BC, allowing the transformation of the Roman Republic into the Empire led by his great-nephew and successor, Caesar Augustus, from 27 BC. Caesar's two political and military memoirs are among the most famous in world literature, appreciated for their heuristic, literary, historical and political value.

Caesar's memoirs may be labelled historical autobiography, where the first-person narrative is not, paradoxically, focused on the author's own life, but on the context in which they have lived. This model will survive throughout history, from the book of the deeds of King James I of Aragon in the mid thirteenth century to the histories of Winston Churchill in the mid twentieth century.[14] The memoirist is usually a politician interested in giving a personal version of events to legitimise their deeds. Credibility emerges from their status as a protagonist or witness of the events narrated. Yet, as Leo Tolstoy states in *War and Peace*, the protagonist of an event is not capable of grasping its whole meaning:

> In historical events we see more plainly than ever the law that forbids us to taste of the fruit of the Tree of Knowledge. It is only unself-conscious activity that bears fruit, and the man who plays a part in an historical drama never understands its significance. If he strives to comprehend it, he is stricken with barrenness.[15]

The narrator of a memoirist history is unable to abstract themselves from their own life and attain sufficient historical perspective to achieve that noble, if also utopian, dream of history: objectivity. Caesar certainly shows with his war memoirs that proximity to the event detracts from his historical perspective and capacity for analysis. Nevertheless, he becomes a reliable source of information that can be used as a primary source of facts, knowledge of which would otherwise never have reached us. In fact, to enhance the *effet de réel* ('reality effect') that Roland Barthes speaks of, Caesar uses the grammatical device of

---

[13] Gaius Julius Caesar, *Commentarii Rerum in Gallia Gestarum*, ed. T. Rice Holmes (Oxford: Scriptorum Classicorum, 1914), Book 1, Chapter 1.

[14] *The Book of Deeds of James I of Aragon*, trans. Damian Smith, Helena Buffery (Burlington: Ashgate, 2003).

[15] Leon Tolstoy, *War and Peace* (New York: Random House, 2012), 1072.

writing in the third person. Although it is evident that author, narrator, protagonist and witness are the same person, this kind of grammatical voice will be used by many other memoirists in the future, from the aforementioned King James I of Aragon to Giambattista Vico and Henry Adams.

Caesar's memoirs also served as a model for the *speculum principum* ('mirror of princes') widely disseminated in the Middle Ages and the Renaissance, from Bede's *Ecclesiastical History of the English People* (731) to Machiavelli's *Prince* (1532). These treatises propose some *exempla* ('examples') of political, military, and moral action for either imitation or avoidance, as other memoirs of rulers selected in this Element such as King Peter IV of Aragon's autobiography show (see Section 2).

Caesar's account of the *Gallic War* and the ensuing civil war is, together with Xenophon's *Hellenica*, the only war account surviving from antiquity whose author was an eyewitness. This makes it of obvious interest as a historical source. But literary critics have also praised the text for its conciseness. Its straightforward style and neat grammar have meant that it has been selected for centuries as compulsory reading in secondary schools for the learning of Latin. The text leaves a certain bitter memory for the high school student who has struggled with its translation. But finally, after a second reading, and beyond a few somewhat rambling passages, its historical insight and heroic dimension can be fully appreciated.

One wonders whether Caesar – or/and his team – was not only a renowned politician but also a outstanding historical author. Most likely he constructed his works helped by a team of editors, but he would have dictated most of the ideas, the main outline and the events to be included in the narrative. Some have argued that its limited and basic vocabulary is explained by the search for a popular audience. But this is less clear, since the number of literate people was already very small. The charm of the work lies rather in its content, in which violent battles, dramatic sieges, daring skirmishes, mysterious portents, mistakes and successes of officers, heroic and cowardly deeds, cruelty and mercy, loyalty and betrayal, and abrupt changes of weather are narrated in detail.

Although not a professional historian, Caesar does not miss any of the basic rules of historical writing. The coordinates of space and time are always present. As the epigraph of this section goes, the Gallic War opens with a programmatic sentence: 'All Gaul is divided into three parts, one of which the Belgae inhabit, the Aquitani another, those who in their own language are called Celts, in our Gauls, the third.'[16] Once the geographical setting has been established, he concisely comments on the main landscape features – mountains, rivers,

---

[16] Caesar, *Commentarii Rerum in Gallia Gestarum,* Book 1, Chapter 1.

plains – that condition their very existence and lead to the expansion that unsettles Rome and generates the first tensions that will lead to war. The narrative proceeds in such detail, combining present and past tense, that it is difficult not to think that Caesar dictated these episodes to his secretaries shortly after the events. At times, the narrative takes on the form of a diary rather than a historical account written after a period of time. This allows it to gain in detail and immediacy, but not to overcome its status as a chronicle.

Caesar is sparing in judgement. He limits himself to narrating events and situations, but very rarely gives his personal interpretation of events or issues praise or criticism. He lets the facts speak for themselves. But the whole air of the narrative suggests that Caesar is more interested in justifying his own performance than in financial gain or personal vanity.

Caesar's historical work – known collectively as the *Commentaries* – is a decisive step for the historical-autobiographical genre. Unlike Sima's auto-biographical writing, his is a deliberately autobiographical and historical book, certainly written in the third person, but designed to tell the witnessed and experienced story. And one to be remembered forever.

Lucian of Samosata's Dream (c. 165)

Dreams work miracles.[17]

Lucian of Samosata (125–181) was a Syrian satirist, rhetorician and sceptic who ridiculed superstition and fideism. He was one of the fully Hellenised Syrians, with an enormous culture, proud of his adopted new language: although his native language was probably Syriac, he wrote in ancient Greek. He was the son of a lower-middle-class family from the city of Samosata, Syria. Overcoming family pressure, he took the decision to devote his life to study and writing instead of sculpture and became a versatile, subversive and multifaceted author. He received his education in Ionia and start travelling throughout the Roman Empire giving lectures. Around the 160s, he settled down in Athens, where he wrote most of his surviving works. Around the 170s, he served as a government official in Egypt, after which point he disappears from the historical record.

Lucian is a typical Imperial Roman citizen but also a Greek-language writer, proud of his cosmopolitan Alexandrian culture. A convinced sophist, impenitent humourist, relentless judge and versatile intellectual, he conveyed through his works the need for literary and historical criticism that would sift the valuable from the superficial, the rational from the superstitious. Along with Dionysius of Halicarnassus, he is one of the few 'history critics' of antiquity. His *How to Write*

---

[17] Lucian of Samosata, *The Dream of Lucian* (London: Gale ECCO, Print Edition, 2010).

History is one of the first epistemological reflections on the discipline and historical criticism. In this treatise, he criticises the historical methodology used by Herodotus and other historians who wrote descriptions of events they had never actually seen. The historian should never exaggerate his stories to entertain his audience, and should be committed to accuracy and precision. He proposes Thucydides as a model of a reliable and accurate historian instead.

In his autobiographical *Dream*, written around 165, Lucian uses the technique of the sleeping vision to reveal his own life. Dream visions have been used since antiquity to justify an authorial stance that seeks to elide acritical accepted sources of order and truth. In a traditional culture, the occurrence of a dream suggests a communion with the divine, inasmuch as it is not manifestly a product of the dreamer's conscious thoughts, and thus the product of dreaming is distinguished from that of active invention or imagination. Few authors could claim the authority to recount their life through a dream as did this highly original and unclassifiable historian, deemed 'inimitable' by Gibbon.

The *Dream* relates the crucial decision of Lucian's life: the choice between a career as a sculptor – pursuing a manual craft – or as an intellectual. Lucian fought hard not to be drawn into the seemingly nondescript life of the craftsmen. In a simple but sophisticated way, he argues that intellectual labour is superior to manual.

Lucian tells how, one day shortly after he left school, his father started discussing his future with some friends. Most of them concluded that higher education would require hard work, a lot of time, considerable expense and ambition for a privileged social position, which contrasted with the moderate position of his family. By contrast, learning a manual profession would have an almost immediate payoff and soon bring in funds for the family. Finally, it was decided that he would enter his maternal uncle's sculpture workshop. Lucian began working there with enthusiasm and dedication, but soon realised he was not cut out for it. On his first day at work, he broke a sculpture through clumsiness, and returned home in tears and despair. After being comforted by his mother – who promised to intercede with her brother – he fell into a deep sleep.

He then had a vision, like the one Homer recounts in the *Iliad* (2, 56): 'A god-sent vision appeared unto me in my slumber out of immortal night.' Two women began to pull him, each in her direction, to the point where he feared he would be torn in half. Each continued to pull in her own direction. The strongest of them, verging on the masculine and with her hands covered in calluses, pressed him to continue his sculpting work. The other, beautiful, splendidly dressed and innately dignified, introduced herself as Education and argued that, even if Lucian managed to reach the sublime level of sculptors like Phidias or Polyclitus, society would always consider him a man who works and lives by his hands, a mere mechanic.

The woman exhorted him by presenting the case of Socrates, who started out as a sculptor but ended up turning to philosophy and thus gaining immortality. If he chose her, he would receive all knowledge, his soul would be adorned with the most sublime virtues and he could aspire to supreme beauty:

> For these are the truly flawless jewels of the soul. Nothing that came to pass of old will escape you, and nothing that must now come to pass; you will even foresee the future with me. In a word, I shall speedily teach you everything that there is, whether it pertains to the gods or to man.[18]

Hearing these persuasive arguments, he opted for Education. Then he saw how the body of the woman who represented Sculpture saddened, became mute, stiffened and finally turned to stone. At this point, Lucian recognises the natural incredulity of the reader, but urges them to bear in mind that 'dreams work miracles'.[19] Education, on the other hand, was delighted and invited him into a celestial chariot pulled by Pegasus-like winged horses. The chariot rose, and allowed him to see from a height what he would have missed if he had not chosen the intellectual vocation: the praise and applause of huge crowds. When he returned to land, he found himself wrapped in a purple robe, with his father watching him affectionately and nodding at the choice he had made. Lucian dreamed, as did Xenophon and Emperor Heraclius.

> Lucian's peculiar autobiographical dream encourages his fellow historians in all eras to aspire to a morally higher life, sacrificing a life of public fame for the work of a historian. It was a forerunner of similar dilemmas faced by later historians in the twentieth century: Richard Pipes decided to renounce an important office in Reagan's administration to resume his academic position at Harvard;[20] Carolyn Steedman's autobiography is a strenuous effort not to lose sight of her intellectual vocation, despite the tragic circumstances she had to live through (Section 5); Gerda Lerner struggled all her life to become a writer to the point of exhaustion, and finally found her calling as a historian (Section 5). All these examples show that, despite its apparent simplicity and assumed fictionality through delivery in the form of a dream, Lucian's autobiography is an extraordinary literary artefact capable of leading us to reflect on our essential life choices, especially in the intellectual and historiographical field.

2 Medieval Narratives

Geoffrey of Villehardouin, King Peter, Ibn Khaldun

Critics agree that autobiography was not a 'natural genre' in the Middle Ages because chronicles contain both historical and imaginative stories, whereas

---

[18] Lucian, *Dream*, 225.   [19] Lucian, *Dream*, 228.
[20] Richard Pipes, *Vixi: Memoirs of a Non-belonger* (New Haven: Yale University Press, 2003), 211.

conventional autobiography technically excludes invention to foreground referentiality.[21] In addition, medieval historical texts tend to include the distant past, whereas autobiography focuses on the span of one person's life. Finally, autobiography was an 'intimate' genre – too subjective, emotional and personal to be understood and practised by medieval chroniclers. Indeed, some scholars have ultimately based their scepticism about medieval auto-biographies on the argument that conventions of the medieval world – such as the limited power of the authorial voice – were not propitious for this kind of personal writing.

Yet this belief in the limitations of the authorial voice in the Middle Ages is contradicted by the existence of some autobiographical and first-person narra-tives such as Abelard's celebrated *Historia Calami Tatum* (c. 1132) and the three cases I present in this section, among others. These authors choose specific metaphors to explain themselves and give coherence to what they want to emphasise in doing so. I argue for a more contextualised idea of autobiography, challenging anachronistic formalist idealism and prescriptive definitions of autobiography to deploy current critical frames that allow us to approach these texts in useful ways. The interest lies in how *historical* writers such as those included in this section wrote about themselves before modern autobiog-raphy was culturally encoded, rather than uncovering medieval autobiographies as forerunners of contemporary practice of the genre.

The three memoirs selected for this section are the crusade memoir of the French knight Geoffrey of Villehardouin (1213), the political autobiography of the Catalan king Peter IV of Aragon (1375), and the travel memoir by the Arab Ibn Khaldun (1405). As in the cases chosen for antiquity, these authors do not have a direct autobiographical purpose since their primary objective is the legitimisation of, respectively, the idea of crusade by a knight, political actions by a king, and personal actions by an official. But all of them *use* autobiographical accounts to gain these objectives: Geoffrey's heroic chron-icle is the testimony of a knight who risked his life for his faith, King Peter's political memoirs include the reflections of a realistic and calculating polit-ician, and Ibn Khaldun's travel memoirs function as the personal narrative of an intellectual who learns from his experiences. Their autobiographies repre-sent three essential types in medieval society: the knight, the ruler and the intellectual.

---

[21] On autobiography in the Middle Ages: Paul Zumthor, 'Autobiographie au Moyen Age?' in *Langue, texte, énigme*, ed. Paul Zumthor (Paris: Seuil, 1975), 165–180; Jean-Claude Schmitt, *La conversion d'Hermann le Juif. Autobiographie, histoire et fiction* (Paris: Seuil, 2003); Jaume Aurell, *Authoring the Past: History, Autobiography and Politics in Medieval Catalonia* (Chicago: University of Chicago Press, 2012).

Geoffrey of Villehardouin's Memoires of Crusade (c. 1213)

> *And because this indulgence was so great,*
> *the hearts of men were much moved,*
> *and many took the cross*
> *for the greatness of the pardon.*[22]

Geoffrey de Villehardouin's (1150–1213) crusade memoir is the first best-seller among historians' autobiographies. Its author was a French nobleman and chronicler who was born in the Castle of Villehardouin, near Troyes (France). He was in the service of his lord, Count Theobald III of Champagne. When Theobald left for the Fourth Crusade in 1199, Geoffrey followed him and sold his goods to the surrounding abbeys to provide himself with resources. During those years, until the conquest of Constantinople by the Western crusaders, he was present at many of the political negotiations that preceded and followed it. This made him the protagonist and an authoritative witness in his memoir of conquest and crusade with a broad knightly content.

Geoffrey wrote his chronicle of the Fourth Crusade, *On the Conquest of Constantinople*, between 1207 and 1213. He used archival documentation to complement his personal testimony of what he had seen with his own eyes. The use of documentation external to memory is a very peculiar and specific feature of historians' autobiographies, also used earlier by Caesar and then by other later examples collected in this Element, from King Peter in the fourteenth century to the more recent Anne Kriegel (*C'est que j'ai cru comprendre*, 1991), Eric Hobsbawm (*Interesting Times*, 2002), and Gerda Lerner (*Fireweed*, 2003). They explicitly acknowledge that they are using documentary sources to complement and make objective their fragile memory. These autobiographical historians reconcile the formal constraints of the genre they are practising with their historical mentality, which makes them seek external legitimisation for their assertions.

Geoffrey was not a professional historian but a knight interested in knowing and writing about the past to provide his personal interpretation of it. Contrary to the uses of the time, he wrote in French rather than Latin, which increased the audience and linguistic value of his chronicle as well, since it made it one of the first works of French prose. He falls into the category of 'history-maker' in the dual sense of being a protagonist of history and writing about it, providing unique primary sources for the relevant events being narrated.

---

[22] Geoffrey de Villehardouin, *Memoirs or Chronicle of the Fourth Crusade and the Conquest of Constantinople*, ed. Frank T. Marzials (London: J. M. Dent, 1908), 2.

The chronicle describes the events between 1198 and 1207. The central event is the 1204 conquest of Constantinople by the Western crusaders, one of the most dramatic events Christianity has ever experienced. What was to be a joint project between the monarchies of Western Christianity and the Empire of Byzantium to reclaim the holy places ended up as a bloodbath in the city of Constantinople. The economic interests of Venice and the lust for power of some continental knights diverted the crusade towards eastern Christendom. The wounds generated by this event have never fully healed, creating an emotional and religious distance between Western Catholicism and eastern Orthodoxy that persists till today.

As with those in Caesar's memoirs, Geoffrey's descriptions are highly meticulous and always select the most picturesque details. His literary style is also reminiscent of Caesar's: concise, direct, leaning more towards grammatical coordination than subordination, very conservative in his use of adjectives and without the tendency to great exaggeration typical of the chronicles of the time. Like Caesar and later Henry Adams too, he uses the third person to achieve a greater impression of distance from the facts but, interestingly, he combines it with the first-person plural – as we have found in the *Acts of the Apostles* in antiquity. Yet he omits some essential information that we have learned from other sources, especially relating to the cruelty of the crusader conquests and the reasons that led the crusaders to deviate from their main objective: the Holy Land.

Geoffrey belongs to a generation of chroniclers who practised a new history with a highly personal, subjective, memoiristic and autobiographical component, such as Robert of Clari, Jean of Joinville, Philippe of Novare, the Byzantine official Niketas Choniates and King James I of Aragon. These new accounts returned to the more personal and testimonial style of classical antiquity, writing about events they had witnessed and participated in, replacing the collective and detached monastic authorship of the previous centuries. With this development, while the traditional chroniclers' work of compilation continued, the function of the 'author' became considerably stronger, since in these new texts the authors serve as both witness and protagonist of their own accounts. Robert of Clari defines this new spirit at the beginning of his chronicle:

> You have heard the truth about the conquest of Constantinople [. . .] for the knight Robert of Clari, who was there, who saw and heard what went on, bears witness to it; he had the conditions of its conquest set down in writing in a truthful fashion. And although he has not related this conquest as elegantly as many a clever storyteller might, in any case he has told nothing but the truth, and there are many things he has left unsaid because he could not relate everything.[23]

---

[23] Michel Zink, *The Invention of Literary Subjectivity* (Baltimore: The Johns Hopkins University Press, 1999), 187–188.

The author's authority derives from his position as witness and participant, which would hardly have been accepted by the earlier medieval tradition of historiography, from late antiquity to the twelfth century, from Eusebius (fourth century) and Bede (eighth century) to the monastic *Grandes Chroniques de France* (thirteenth century). All of these new memorialist chroniclers recount 'what has happened' solely from the point of view of 'what happened to them'. Their chronicles were deliberately written in prose, which appears to guarantee referentiality and serves, moreover, to anticipate criticism that might be aimed at writers who were not strictly speaking 'men of letters' but 'men of arms'. The figure of the soldier-writer, knight-historian and king-chronicler emerged from this generation of prose writers, a cultural type to see continuity in the following centuries, and to which Winston Churchill would be a worthy epilogue in the twentieth century.

This type of testimonial history is necessarily a history of the present time, which contrasts completely with other historical genres previously practiced during the Middle Ages, such as chronological annals, genealogies, national and universal histories. These *old* histories were promoted by monarchs to consolidate the memory of their kingdom and legitimise domination of their territory, all of them systematically referring to a remote past that is convenient to mythologise. Geoffrey's autobiographical account epitomises the birth of a new genre, one that seeks to broaden the audience and avoid excessive dependence on ecclesiastical or civil patrons. While the old history was a monastic, compiled and anonymous team effort, Geoffrey's chronicle is a work with strong authorial authority: lay, individual, subjective and autobiographical.

King Peter of Aragon's Political Autobiography (1375)

> *We bore a golden sceptre with a ruby*
> *on the top in the right hand*
> *and a golden orb with a cross of pearls*
> *and precious stones in the left,*
> *and we had a sword covered with pearls*
> *and precious stones belted on.*[24]

Peter IV (1319–1387) was the king of the Crown of Aragon, one of the most largest and powerful kingdoms of Europe at that time. His long reign of fifty-one years, his military skills and his political ambition allowed him to consolidate the Crown of Aragon as the main geopolitical power in the western Mediterranean. But he was a giant with feet of clay, because the expansion he launched was immensely costly. To partly alleviate this problem, the king had to

---

[24] Peter IV of Aragon, *Chronicle. Pere III of Catalonia (Pedro IV of Aragon)*, eds. Mary Hillgarth and Jocelyn N. Hillgarth (Toronto: Pontifical Institute, 1980), I: 281–282.

seek various procedures to reinforce and legitimise his authority, among which were the consolidation of the chancellery, the proliferation of royal rituals (hence his nickname 'the Ceremonious'), the performance of the transgressive ceremony of self-coronation when he was only seventeen, the attraction of many astrologers to his court and, crucially, the writing of his long and detailed autobiography.

The function of his political memoir, like those of Caesar and his great-grandfather King James the Conqueror before him, and that of Winston Churchill long after, is clearly exemplary:

> Therefore, as king, reigning over the kingdom of Aragon by His [God's] splendid clemency, we have thought and wished to leave a record of them [the deeds of his reign] in writing, and to make a book. We wish this not for Our arrogance and glory, but so that the Kings, Our successors, on reading this book and hearing that We, by firm hope and faith and patience, which We had in the great goodness and mercy of Our Creator, have passed through divers perils and many wars with powerful enemies, and have been delivered with great honor and victory, should take this as an example.[25]

Some readers of this Element are probably familiar with the popular *Game of Thrones*. They will remember the terrible scene in which Khal Drogo, the chief of the Dothraki dynasty, invites his rival Vyseris, brother of Princess Daenerys, to negotiate some issues at his court, in an apparently diplomatic and peaceful visit. At an unexpected moment, Drogo pours incandescent molten gold over Vyseris' head. He agonises in spasmodic convulsions, writhing in pain. He has pretended to be king, and Drogo has promised him from the beginning that he himself will crown him. And he keeps his promise in this macabre and grisly way.

When I saw the scene, I thought that, once again, reality surpasses fiction: I remembered what I had read in Peter the Ceremonious' autobiography. Peter did not follow the macabre tradition of pouring incandescent gold on the head of his adversary, as seems to have been done in the Roman Empire. He found a crueller one, making some nobles who had rebelled against him swallow the molten bronze of the bells they used to summon their meetings. Far from trying to hide his cruelty, King Peter wanted this scene to appear in his autobiography, precisely to increase the respect of his subjects and the memory of posterity. The *Llibre* includes other stories which unambiguously reflect Peter's authority and cruelty. He writes of how he ordered condemned men to be dragged by horses before being hanged; he pressured officials into executing several criminals before they could take advantage of the reprieve as a consequence of his marriage; he justifies the assassination of his stepbrother Ferran with incredible coldness.

---

[25] Peter IV, *Chronicle*, 131–132.

Peter worked on his political memoirs between 1375 and 1386. It is a self-portrait of a tormented king, surrounded by military threats, troubled by the lack of internal unity within his realm, menaced by a major economic crisis, shocked by the epidemic of the Black Death, and – paradoxically – convinced of his providential function as the leader of an emergent modern state. The text reflects an era in which the old medieval structures based on territorial and feudal conceptions of the monarchy had to confront new political tendencies, specifically the consolidation of monarchical authority. A new historical context demanded a renewed historical text, a revised form of representing the past. Peter's autobiography is a brilliant example of a political treatise, a *speculum principum*, written by a late medieval king with the mindset of a Renaissance prince.

Peter is not a knight-king who extends the territories of his kingdom with his conquests against the infidels, but an administrator who plans the campaign and organises a team of royal scribes to preserve the history of the kingdom's deeds: we can still find in the Barcelona archives the correspondence in which he instructs his scribes on how to write his memoirs. For instance, he wrote a letter to one of his scribes, Bernat Descoll, asking him that, in a chapter on the negotiations between the king and Venice, he should emphasise some deeds the king wants recorded in detail, day by day:

> what persons and how many passed with us to Sardinia, after En Bernat de Cabrera had vanquished the Genoese fleet and taken Alghero, and then the rebellion of Alghero, *as you sketched it out for us*. And also make mention of where we reembarked and where we landed and afterwards what happened to us, *day by day*, and of who died there and with whom we returned, as clearly as you can, and in detail.[26]

The explanation of the nature of this kind of authorship may well come also from the Iberian king Alfonso el Sabio of Castile (Alfonso the Wise), who explains in his delightful Spanish:

> We often say: the King makes a book, not because he writes it with his own hands but because he composes the subjects, corrects them and adds a new nuance and rectifies them and shows the way they should be done, and they are written thus under his instructions and we say then that the King makes the book. Similarly when we say the King builds a palace or does some other work, it is not because he does so with his own hands but because he orders it to be built and he provides everything required to make it so.[27]

---

[26] This amazing letter, dated 8 August 1375, is perhaps the most explicit medieval document that describes the manner of writing royal history in the Middle Ages: English edition in *Chronicle. Pere III of Catalonia (Pedro IV of Aragon)*, eds. Mary Hillgarth and Jocelyn N. Hillgarth (Toronto: Pontifical Institute of Mediaeval Studies, 1980), II: 606–609. The emphases are mine.

[27] Antonio G. Solalinde, 'Intervención de Alfonso X en la redacción de sus obras', *Revista de Filología Española* II (1915): 286.

In the chronicle, the king aims to appear primarily as a ruler rather than as a knight, and stories of military action are replaced by theoretical ruminations on political strategy and ideological legitimisation. He hardly ever participates in battles, because he functions as a statesman not a soldier. His meticulous and Machiavellian use of personal memory and collective chancellery documentation exhibits his despotic regal ambition. He harnesses historical writing as a platform for political self-legitimisation and self-representation. If we follow the Weberian categories, in the absence of legal legitimisation, the medieval king had to create new forms of charismatic legitimisation, the compilation of his memoirs being one of the most significant.

Peter created, through this autobiographical chronicle, the new image of the monarchy that his troubled times required. His account presents a succession of ideas, concepts and values in contrast to Geoffrey's narration of stories. He shows that the recounting of one's life may become an efficient weapon for justifying and legitimising politics. He provides an exceptional source of political theory and practice in the Middle Ages and, in consonance with the coming Renaissance, he uses his autobiography as a political treatise.

Peter's autobiography lies halfway between Caesar's war memoirs and Machiavelli's later political treatise. Its elaboration is a team effort with the chancellery officials as opposed to a personal authorship where the imagination can run its course freely, or the traditional compilations of Benedictine abbeys. The king would give outline instructions to his officers, who would then complete the drafting for the king's final approval. Peter is shown as the head of a pre-modern state rather than a knight like his great-grandfather James the Conqueror or the crusading chroniclers reviewed in the previous section. He is a sedentary king, with the court already settled in Barcelona, rather than a knight-king with his court moving according to military needs. He acts as a figure of the imperial mood of his successors, the emperors Charles V and Philip II of Spain.

Ibn Khaldun's Travel Memoir (1405)

Since my early childhood,
I have never ceased to be interested in acquiring
the science of the good qualities of the soul.[28]

Ibn Khaldun (1332–1406) is the author of a great historical and sociological work, *Muqaddimah* ('Introduction to Universal History'). He is admired as

---

[28] Ibn Jaldun, *Autobiografía y Viajes a través de Occidente y Oriente*, ed. Mostapha Jarmouni (Granada: Universidad de Granada, 2018), 85.

a social science forerunner capable of moving through such diverse disciplines as geography, sociology, economics and demography. His family came from the south of Arabia, although later they moved to Seville, Ceuta and Tunis, where Ibn Khaldun was born. His life was full of difficulties. He lost his parents to the Black Death in 1348 and his family (wife and children) in a shipwreck in 1384.

The narrative structure of his autobiography is quite conventional. He begins by recounting the distant, almost legendary, origins of his family, from the time of Muhammad. His ancestors belonged to an Arab tribe from Hadhramaut (Yemen) and moved to the Iberian Peninsula around the eighth century, at the tome of the Islamic conquest. Then, he focuses on his birth and early life, emphasising his education the study of the Koran and the Arabic language. Once he completed his studies, he was appointed *waly* ('chancellor') in Tunis. He travelled from there throughout the Maghreb, which he got to know at first hand. His narration then focuses on his trip to Al-Andalus, landing in Gibraltar and moving thence to Granada, to which he would return a few years later. He details some of his pilgrimages to Mecca from Cairo. In 1383, he finally resettled in Cairo, where he found greater stability in his life and studies. The narrative ends in 1405, with an uncertain future, since Ibn Khaldun claims that 'is Allah who holds the future of things in His hands!'

The portrait we get of Ibn Khaldun from his autobiography is of a very active man, engaged in many political and diplomatic actions. However, in the second part of his life, after resettling in Cairo, he was allowed to devote himself more steadily to study and teaching. These were serene and happy years, because he was finally able to dedicate himself to composing his works, something that brought him into harmony with himself, as he recognises in his autobiography. This is a state of soul – writing as therapy – that many of the authors analysed in this Element share. Writing is an arduous process but, in the end, it responds most of the time to an inner impulse that cannot be repressed, despite the difficulties encountered along the way. Although Ibn Khaldun lived at a time when historians were not yet professionals, his perfectionism has the detail and systematics of a meticulous observer of the past.

Ibn Khaldun demonstrates that autobiography also has a historiographical function. His travel memoir is closely connected to his great historical work, *Muquaddima* (1377). Both have *etiology* as their main axis, the study of the causes of history, especially the decline of civilisations, of what makes them languish, die and disappear. The spirit of Ibn Khaldun seems to have been revived centuries later with Gibbon's autobiography, discussed in this Element.

Ibn Khaldun emerges as a pioneering and restless scholar, at the crossroads of humanities and social sciences. He combines his political with his intellectual personality, action with contemplation, diplomatic activity with academia, public officialdom with private interest, the writing of objective essays with that of personal autobiographies. Nothing escapes his intellectual curiosity.

In addition, Ibn Khaldun's memoir is a good example of travel literature in autobiographical form, a subgenre practised since antiquity by scientists such as the Greek geographer Pausanias and later by the celebrated eighteenth-century diarists James Cook and Alexander von Humboldt, enjoying enormous popularity in nineteenth-century Romanticism. Ibn Khaldun had probably read the mythical voyages of Marco Polo, popularised in the West during the previous century. Already by modernity, especially during the Romantic era, autobiographical travel literature had expanded significantly, with authors such as Joseph Conrad, Herman Melville, David Livingstone, Thomas Edward Lawrence, Jules Verne, Ernest Hemingway, Robert D. Kaplan and Alexandra David-Néel.

Since the *Odyssey* of Homer, the journey has always been considered an image of life itself, with its obstacles, difficulties, challenges and conquests. The *Grand Tour*, habitually through the vestiges of classical culture on the Mediterranean shore, was a mandatory part of the curriculum of European elites until quite recently. Travel forms, forges, and matures character. One cannot but draw parallels between Ibn Khaldun and his predecessor Dante, whose exile served to conclude his sublime *Divine Comedy*, and with modern historians turned autobiographers included in this Element such as Gibbon, Adams and Lerner.

Ibn Khaldun shows that travel literature comes naturally to historians, since they have a special sensitivity to capturing the most relevant details of each new society they meet, and are also endowed with a particular inclination towards precision and realism. Moreover, the journey is a metaphor for life, which fits perfectly with the typical characteristics of the autobiographical genre. Beyond his somewhat rambling writing, Ibn Khaldun has left us an early proof of the testimonial, didactic and historical value of travel literature.

3 Western Rationalities

Giambattista Vico, Edward Gibbon, Henry Adams

During early modernity in the West, autobiography was a spiritual genre, taking the Life of St. Teresa as a model, and also appearing in diary form.[29] But in the specific field of historians' autobiographies, its golden age came from the eighteenth century onwards. Giambattista Vico's *Life of Giambattista Vico Written by Himself* (1731), Edward Gibbon's *Memoirs of My Life* (1796) and Henry Adams' *The Education of Henry Adams* (1918) are the classic foundational texts of this

---

[29] James Amelang, *The Flight of Icarus. Artisan Autobiography in Early Modern Europe* (Stanford: Stanford University Press, 1998).

genre of historians' autobiographies in the West. Although Adams was the only professional historian among them, they are clearly identified with the historical discipline, and their work left a very deep mark in the philosophy of history (Vico), the historical monograph (Gibbon) and the historical essay (Adams). Their autobiographies are, therefore, relevant platforms situated at the threshold of the professionalisation of history experienced in the West during the first half of the twentieth century.

At the same time, these three memoirs work as different models of autobiographical writing among successive historians. Vico created a narrative model to convey the passion of a life dedicated to study. He is the forerunner of the autobiographies of humanists as practised by Benedetto Croce, Robin Collingwood and Eric Voegelin in the twentieth-century interwar period. Gibbon replicated Vico's model, but added a specific historiographical orientation, which would be taken up by other important historians of the mid twentieth century, notably Richard Pipes, Eric Hobsbawm and Annie Kriegel. Adams is the most all-encompassing of the three, introducing intellectual and professional events as well as intimate and familial ones into his personal testimony. His autobiography expanded the specifically intellectual and historiographical memoir to the whole field of historical understanding from the account of one's own life. His model connects more to the autobiographies of women such as Carolyn Steedman, Jill Conway and Gerda Lerner, with their more integrated style – that is, not limited to the professional or academic – or to postmodern historians such as Carlos Eire and Robert A. Rosenstone at the end of the twentieth century.

Apart from their role as prestigious and influential historians, the renown of Vico, Gibbon and Adams comes from their ability to address universal issues through their autobiographical accounts. They have a central place in the establishment and evolution of modern historians' autobiographical writing, and even of autobiography in general. The power of these texts derives from the fact that their authors are pre-eminently historians. This specific intellectual training, disciplinary orientation and sustained interest in the study of human experience in the past led them to an original approach in writing their own lives. They find connections between the experience of life, the writing of history and the autobiographical project. Reading their life stories, one realises how their training as historians conditions their autobiographical authorial intention.

Other parallels can also be drawn between the autobiographies of the three historians reviewed in this section.[30] Vico's and Gibbon's are an inescapable intellectual testament to the European Enlightenment. From a formal and

---

[30] Jeremy D. Popkin, *History, Historians & Autobiography* (Chicago: The University of Chicago Press, 2005), 92–119.

grammatical perspective, Vico's and Adams' are written in the third person, creating an ostensible – and somewhat artificial – distance between the author and his narrated character. This apparent detachment, however, is highly effective in terms of the intellectual artefact that these historians aim to create.

All three historians have ennobled history, since their influence extends far beyond the boundaries of the discipline. They have a privileged place in some of the most influential intellectual trends of modernity, constituting essential referents of historicism (Vico), Enlightenment (Gibbon) and modernism (Adams).

Giambattista Vico's Intellectual Autobiography (1731)

They should first apprehend, then judge, and finally reason.[31]

Around 1725, Vico received a memorandum entitled 'Proposal to the Scholars of Italy', drawn up by Count Gian Artico di Porcia. Vico and other Italian scholars were asked to submit an autobiographical account that would be used for the edification of young students and the reform of Italian school curricula and methods. Only Vico responded to this invitation. Based on the guidelines of Artico's proposal and on his own intellectual agenda, he prepared an account of his life, lineage and education, pointing out the strong and the weak points of the curriculum on which he had been educated. The result is a clever intellectual autobiography that, for all its dense and tortured prose, has been much appreciated by literary critics in particular and scholars in general.

Giambattista Vico (1660–1744) spent his entire life in Naples. The sixth of eight children, his family always struggled financially, but the work of his father – a book dealer – allowed him to spend long hours in deep reading from a very young age. He had several Jesuit teachers but was essentially self-taught. This autodidactic education, which will be replicated in most of the following historian-autobiographers such as Gibbon, Adams and Lerner, consisted of reading the Greek and Roman classics, jurisprudence and philosophical-scholastic studies. This solid and interdisciplinary base allowed him to venture into questions of philosophy of science: he has enjoyed a posthumous and prolonged celebrity thanks to his treatise *New Science* (1725), in which he proposed a systematic unification of the humanities to achieve a reliable method for the study of all civilisations, as well as their cycles of rise and decline.[32]

His autobiography takes the form of a kind of intellectual remembrance: the authors he has admired or rejected, the works he has published, the process of

---

[31] Giambattista Vico, *The Autobiography of Gaimbattista Vico*, eds. Max Harold Fisch and Thomas Goddard Bergin (Ithaca: Cornell University Press, 1995), 124.

[32] Benedetto Croce, *The Philosophy of Giambattista Vico* (New York: Russell and Russell, 1964).

writing them, the sources he used, the criticism and praise he received, his defence, the confession of some errors, what he would now retract, and defending only what seems defensible after due consideration.[33] Vico's autobiographical project, and the external impulse he received to write it, prefigures the twentieth-century French *ego-historians* such as Georges Duby, Jacques Le Goff and Emmanuel Le Roy Ladurie, who resisted writing their intellectual memoirs until another respected intellectual – Pierre Nora – launched a common project. The result are memoirs focused on – and reduced to – the intellectual sphere, with the personal or emotional appearing only very marginally, and always as a complement to the intellectual vicissitudes that follow.

Vico begins his narration with the frightening accident he suffered as a child. He fell down a stairwell and hit his head so hard that he was unconscious for hours. But, almost miraculously, it did not affect his spine. After a three-year recovery period, which left him with chronic pain and many ups and downs in his body and mind, Vico was motivated to dedicate himself to intellectual adventure. Perhaps as a result of this accident, he always moved between melancholy and moments of great intellectual exaltation. Between 1686 and 1695, he worked as a tutor to the Rocca family in Vatolla – a town about a hundred kilometres from Naples – dedicating himself to all kinds of reading: from Plato to Virgil, Dante to Petrarch. In 1699, he was appointed Professor of Aesthetics at the University of Naples. The authors who most influenced him during this period were Plato, Tacitus, Grotius and Bacon. Overlooked for the law professorship that was his initial intention, he devoted himself with greater zeal to philosophy, publishing his influential *Scienza Nuova*. He spent the last years of his life nostalgically, with the anxiety of not having seen his work recognised, something that would only happen long after his death, when he came to be considered a hero by nineteenth-century historicists and Marxists and twentieth-century influential scholars such as Isaiah Berlin, Edward Said and Hayden White.

Vico's autobiography functions as an exemplary historical and literary narrative, historical source, intellectual history and historiographical artefact. It can be considered an *interventional* autobiography, since it not only sets out to describe and analyse certain intellectual issues that it was his lot to experience, but also to 'intervene' in that debate. The author seeks to convey that any approach to knowledge requires an interdisciplinary approach and critical mind, going beyond excessive specialisation and acritical submission.

---

[33] Peter Burke, *Vico* (Oxford: Oxford University Press, 1985); Donald P. Verene, *The New Art of Autobiography: An Essay on the Life of Giambattista Vico Written by Himself* (Oxford: Clarendon, 1991); Donald P. Verene, *Philosophy and the Return to Self-Knowledge* (New Haven: Yale University Press, 1997).

Vico writes in an unsystematic way, making the reading of his autobiography somewhat arduous. But he manages to leave a deep impression on his readers, and it is not surprising that he has been considered – albeit belatedly – one of the most persuasive Western thinkers. One of the keys to his intellectual attraction – and perhaps to his late reception – is his ability to interact with various disciplines, using his most representative authors as references. He highlights Plato as a reference in philosophy and the speculative way of proceeding, Tacitus as a reference in history and the approach to reality, Francis Bacon for scientific research, and Hugo Grotius as a reference for natural and universal law. His autobiography is a method of scientific introspection, revealing the entrails of intellectual production.

Just as he might be said to have created a 'new science' with his classical work on human understanding, he also created a 'new art of autobiography' with his personal account. Benedetto Croce, his successor in Naples as intellectual and historiographical referent in the twentieth century, stated that Vico's autobiography is the projection and application of the *Scienza Nuova* to the life of its author, the course of his own intellectual history. While the elements of Descartes' autobiography in the *Discourse of Method* were simply segments of an existence added to give the theory a setting, Vico deliberately inserts his method in the *Autobiography*. His autobiography therefore has not only intellectual but also specific historiographical value, since he contributed to the specification of the historical discipline among other sciences.

While arguing for the central importance of self-knowledge as a key incentive for the knowledge of all other disciplines, he did more to emancipate history from theology, politics and morals than any previous philosopher of history. He gave his own autobiography a central place as an account in the history of the mind. Self-knowledge become then one of the foundations of scientific knowledge and led to a more comprehensible approach to reality. Vico took advantage of the ability to explore human experience – *a* personal story – in order to comprehend the processes and general laws that govern historical evolution and historical narration. In the end, he created a kind of intellectual autobiography which involved the application of the introspective method by an original thinker to his own thought.

Edward Gibbon's Historical Autobiography (1795)

The discipline and evolution of a modern battalion
gave me a clearer notion of the Phalanx and the Legion,
and the Captain of the Hampshire grenadiers
has not been useless to the historian of the Roman Empire.[34]

---

[34] Edward Gibbon, *Memories of My Life*, ed. Georges A. Bonnard (New York: Funk and Wagnalls, 1966), 117.

These words illustrate the great historiographical authority of the author of *Decline and Fall of the Roman Empire*, who was able to recognise in the present the imprints of the past, and to vivify the past – the history of Roman Empire – with present analogies of and his actual experiences of military service. Some of the data and interpretations of his classic work may have been superseded by subsequent specialist literature, but it is still routinely cited among the classics of historiography and has been a continuing source of inspiration for literary critics, intellectual historians and historians of ideas – such as the six volumes that John Pocock devoted to it in his *Barbarism and Religion*, a phrase coined by Gibbon himself.[35] Gibbon is also a type of Enlightened historian-philosopher, so he represents – with David Hume[36] – a whole generation not only of historians but of Enlightened thinkers. Having his autobiography is therefore a privilege that historians – and intellectuals more generally – cannot disdain.

Edward Gibbon (1737–1794) was an English politician and historian. He was born in Putney, then a town near London. He had red hair, a high-pitched voice and a tendency to obesity that became more pronounced in his maturity, as shown in his portraits. His mother died when he was ten years old, and he lost his five brothers and one sister when they were in their childhood. His father and grandfathers were involved in politics, diplomacy and business. The former sent him to Magdalen College, Oxford, when he was fourteen. But he did not enjoy its ornate and formalist atmosphere, although in his autobiography he notes that it was there that he converted to Catholicism in 1753, after a sceptical youth. He was expelled from Oxford for his conversion, and his father then sent him to Lausanne, Switzerland, where he again lost his faith.

In Lausanne, he found a place of peace and serenity that captivated him all his life, and to which he would repeatedly retire to resume his writing. In 1772 his father died, leaving him enough to live comfortably in London. In 1774, he won a seat in Parliament, where he served for eight years, combining it with the intense historiographical labour of the long writing of *Decline and Fall*. He finished his great book in 1788, in retirement in Lausanne. The French Revolution drove him back to London, where he worked on his autobiography until his death in 1794.

Gibbon is a model of the English Enlightenment, particularly attached to its historiographical dimension. Although he chose knowledge as a vocation from an early age, he always carried this close link to civil society with him. It contributed to the fact that his historical works always had a vivid narrative

---

[35] John G. A. Pocock, *Barbarism and Religion*, 6 vols (Cambridge: Cambridge University Press, 1999–2015).

[36] David F. Norton and Richard H. Popkin, eds., *David Hume: Philosophical Historian* (Indianapolis: Bobbs-Merrill, 1965).

that prevented them from remaining mere archaeological works and projected them into the present. During his life, he suffered many family losses – mother, brothers and sister – as well as setbacks in his health, professional life and fortune. But he never lost his commitment to study and writing, or that touch of healthy humorous irony that pervades his historical writings and, above all, his autobiography.

Beyond its evident autobiographical and historiographical value, Gibbon's *Memories of My Life* has been considered a literary work in its own right. However, it is difficult to single out which of its qualities is so appealing to read. Its prose is dense, its structure fuzzy, and it lacks narrative unity since its author wrote several drafts that modern editors have subsequently compiled. But the intensity and insight with which Gibbon develops his intellectual progress, his pungent epigrams and his brilliant irony compensate for these formal deficiencies. It catches the reader continually thinking about their own dedication to history.

Just as the media today feeds our obsession with obtaining even the most trivial details about major celebrities, Gibbon provides us with an integrated description of all aspects of a historian's life, in which all facets of his existence – from the most intimate and familiar to the most professional and public – are combined. His memoirs also contain information on the formation – a kind of *bildungsroman* – of one of the most representative and influential works of historiography of all time, namely his *Decline and Fall*. He details, for instance, the initial impetus for this book:

> The historian of the *Decline and Fall* must not regret his time of experience [of foreign travel], since it was the view of Italy and Rome which determined the choice of the subject. In my Journal the place and moment of conception are recorded; the fifteenth of October 1764, in the close of evening, as I sat musing in the Church of the Zoccolanti or Franciscan Fryars, while they were singing Vespers in the Temple of Jupiter on the ruins of the Capitol. But my original plan was circumscribed to the decay of the City, rather than on the Empire: and, though my reading and reflections began to point towards the object, some years elapsed, and several avocations intervened before I was seriously engaged in the execution of that laborious work.[37]

Gibbon is the first historian to give us explicit clues to his historiographical production in his autobiography. During the twentieth century, dozens of prominent historians such as Benedetto Croce, Robin Collingwood, Eric Hobsbawm, Jill K. Conway, Gabrielle M. Spiegel, Natalie Z. Davis or Robert A. Rosenstone would use their memoirs to give us clues to the process of elaboration of their

---

[37] Gibbon, *Memories*, 136.

works – information of extraordinary usefulness and interest.[38] But Gibbon was a forerunner in endowing an autobiography with this specifically historiographical dimension.

Gibbon emphasises the value of self-education for historical training: 'In the life of every man of letters, there is an area, a level from whence he soars with his own wings to his proper height, and the most important part of his education is that which he bestows on himself.'[39] He also gives us a description of his own personality, which allows us to get an idea of the qualities that a good historian must possess. The intellectual task is so exciting that it does not allow for slacking off:

> The love of study, a passion which derives fresh vigour from enjoyment, supplies each day, each hour, with a perpetual sources of independent and rational pleasure; and I am not sensible of any decay of the mental faculties. The original soil has been highly improved by labour and cultivation.[40]

Gibbon admits that a comfortable economic position makes possible a life dedicated to study, research and writing. This is the case of the previous storytellers writing autobiography we have already analysed. Until the disciplines became professionalised, historians emerged from families with economic surpluses and with some intellectuals among their ancestors. Henry Adams, our next case study, also responds to these characteristics, but he is also our first professional historian writing an autobiography – and one which became a bestseller and achieved well-deserved fame as a literary classic.

Henry Adams' Biographical Autobiography (1907)

> *Throughout human history*
> *the waste of mind has been appalling,*
> *and, as this story is meant to show,*
> *society has conspired to promote it.*[41]

Henry Adams' *Education* is a classic not only among historians' autobiographies, but also of Western literature.[42] Winner of the Pulitzer Prize in 1919 and acclaimed in some rankings as the best English-language nonfiction book of the

---

[38] Jaume Aurell, 'Benedetto Croce and Robin Collingwood: Historiographic and Humanistic Approaches to the Self and the World', *Prose Studies* 31 (2009): 214–226; Jaume Aurell, 'Performative Academic Careers: Gabrielle Spiegel and Natalie Davis', *Rethinking History* 13.1 (2009): 53–64; Jaume Aurell, 'Autobiographical Texts as Historiographical Sources: Rereading Fernand Braudel and Annie Kriegel', *Biography* 29.3 (2006): 425–445.

[39] Gibbon, *Memories*, 74.   [40] Gibbon, *Memories*, 187.

[41] Henry Adams, *The Education of Henry Adams* (New York: The Modern Library, 1931), 314.

[42] Jacob C. Levenson, *The Mind and Art of Henry Adams* (Stanford: Stanford University Press, 1957); John Carlos Rowe, *Henry Adams and Henry James: The Emergence of a Modern Consciousness* (Ithaca: Cornell University Press, 1976).

twentieth century, his memoirs were a bestseller in their time, like those of Geoffrey in the twelfth century (with the limitations of the pre-print era), Jill K. Conway in the late twentieth century and Carlos Eire in the twenty-first century. Adams designed his *Education* with a limited audience of intellectuals and scholars in mind. But over time the thick volume was systematically included among the most widely read nonfiction books. What could explain this success?

Adams was born in Boston in 1838 and died in Washington in 1918. He came from a distinguished family of American politicians and diplomats. John Adams and John Quincy Adams, the second and sixth presidents of the nation, were included among his direct ancestors. His father, Charles Francis Adams, was the ambassador to England during Abraham Lincoln's presidency. His maternal family had been successfully engaged in business, notably his grandfather Peter Chardon Brooks. In addition, the seven years of his brief but productive experience as a professor of medieval history at Harvard connected him with the intellectual and professional elite of the country. Finally, his fame was preceded by his prolific historical work, including the monumental *The History of the United States of America during the Administrations of Thomas Jefferson and James Madison* (1889–1891) and the acclaimed *Mont Saint-Michel and Chartres* (1904), a somewhat idealised plea for the unity of the medieval world and the sublimity of its cathedrals.

At the age of twenty, after graduating from Harvard, he undertook an initiatory trip to Europe, which he details in his memoirs, just as Ibn Khaldun and Edward Gibbon had done with their travels to Africa and Italy. This led him to study civil law – a sterile and unsuccessful venture if we take him at his word – at the University of Berlin. He then served as secretary to the ambassador to the United Kingdom, a post that had been held by his own father, between 1861 and 1868. There he also acted as an anonymous correspondent for *The New York Times* and befriended some public intellectuals including Charles Lyell, Francis T. Palgrave, Richard Monckton Milnes, Charles Milnes Gaskell and John Stuart Mill, who endowed him with a remarkable attachment to the liberal democratic tradition.

After an interlude as a journalist, he was recruited to teach medieval history at Harvard University, which he did between 1870 and 1877. However, he was never passionate about university teaching or scholarly research. As he states in his autobiography, 'Harvard taught little, and that little ill, but it left the mind open, free from bias, ignorant of facts, but docile.'[43] In his memoirs, those years appear as a parenthesis in his life, somewhat tedious and uncomfortable. Yet his

---

[43] Adams, *Education*, 55.

major contribution to historical studies – and to American university studies in general – was the importation of the seminar method, which he had witnessed in his years in Germany.

Prematurely retired at thirty-nine from diplomatic office and university teaching, the rest of his memoirs are an account of his years of retirement and writing, full of scepticism and melancholy, but also of literary vigour and a good dose of intelligent spark. *The Education* also exudes a certain tone of resentment typical of a member of the social and political elite who does not feel sufficiently valued by the middle class. The last chapter ('Failure') shows a despondent man at the early age of thirty-three. As a professor, 'he regarded himself as a failure'.[44] After his brief stint at Harvard, he declared: 'He quitted the university at last, in 1877, with a feeling that, if it had not been for the invariable courtesy and kindness shown by every one in it, from the President to the injured students, he should be sore at his failure.'[45]

This scepticism is also projected onto the situation of historical studies in his time. It unnerved him that the supposedly scientific discipline founded by the German historicists whose theories he had learned first-hand during his stay in Berlin was bankrupt: 'History had lost even the sense of shame. It was a hundred years behind the experimental sciences. For all serious purposes, it was less instructive than Walter Scott and Alexandre Dumas.'[46] It had achieved neither the attraction of a good literary narrative nor the consistency of the experimental sciences, for which he advocated, as one of the main promoters of that 'noble dream' to which Peter Novick referred, under the claim of the 'general laws of history'.[47] In fact, he tried – unsuccessfully – to give a scientific foundation to the theory of the medieval foundations of American institutions.[48] He proposed applying to history the principles of biological evolution as sketched by Darwin combined with Comtean positivism to promote 'scientific' history following an 'anti-modernist' agenda, as Gabrielle M. Spiegel has argued.[49]

The Education of Henry Adams introduces us for the first time to the American context – where, based on his model, autobiographies of historians proliferated extraordinarily during the twentieth century.[50] These autobiographies illustrate

---

[44] Adams, *Education*, 304.   [45] Adams, *Education*, 305.   [46] Adams, *Education*, 301.

[47] Peter Novick, *That Noble Dream: The 'Objectivity Question' and the American Historical Profession* (Cambridge: Cambridge University Press, 1988), 33.

[48] Dorothy Ross, *The Origins of American Social Science* (Cambridge: Cambridge University Press, 1992), 64. See also William H. Jordy, *Henry Adams: Scientific Historian* (New Haven: Yale University Press, 1952).

[49] Gabrielle M. Spiegel, 'In the Mirror's Eye: The Writing of Medieval History in America', in *Imagined Histories: American Historians Interpret the Past*, eds. Anthony Molho and Gordon S. Wood (Princeton: Princeton University Press, 1998), 238–262.

[50] Albert E. Stone, *Autobiographical Occasions and Original Acts: Versions of American Identity from Henry Adams to Nate Shaw* (Philadelphia: University of Pennsylvania Press, 1982).

the impact of industrialisation, urbanisation and immigration on the traditional agrarian image and experience of American society and to the accompanying dislocations in values, job developments, and gender roles and identities. In the American tradition, and particularly among historians, Benjamin Franklin's *Autobiography* and Henry Adams' *Education* served as arbiters of autobiographical form and moulded the notion of the autobiographical persona.[51] This model would serve not only for the first generation of American historians such as William Langer and Arthur Schlesinger, Sr., who engaged with autobiography biographically, but also for the second generation such as Richard Pipes and Arthur Schlesinger, Jr., who fostered a monographic model. This tendency would shift during the 1990s for a third generation that included figures such as the postmodern Carlos Eire and Robert A. Rosenstone referred to in Section 6.

As seen in these genealogies, Adams' autobiography became not only a model for Western literature but more specifically for historians. After the experience of Vico, Gibbon and Adams, any intellectual – and, of course, any historian – felt authorised to write their intellectual memoirs. Autobiography would no longer be seen as an unconventional genre, but as an orthodox means of conveying the type of historical reflection and story that could hardly have been exposed through the rigid methodologies of conventional historical genres. The following cases confirm this reality.

4 Colonisation Perplexities

Fukuzawa Yukichi, Taha Hussein, Gu Jiegang, Nirad Chaudhuri

This section covers four great nations which embody entire civilisations, namely China (Gu Jiegang), India (Nirad C. Chaudhuri), Japan (Fukuzawa Yukichi) and Islamic Egypt (Taha Hussein). The four corresponding memoiristic historians share the same drama: the effects of colonisation and industrialisation, the tension between tradition and modernisation, and the dilemma between indigenous traditions and the reality imposed by British, Dutch and French colonialism. They all belong to the chronological period between the mid nineteenth and mid twentieth centuries.

Crucially, these four historians turned autobiographers were interested in analysing the original sources and authorities of their respective civilisations. And they did so in a critical way, unimpressed by the self-imposed conclusions of the ancestral traditions of their respective civilisations – the Chinese, Hindu and Japanese heuristic traditions in the case of Gu, Chaudhuri, and Fukuzawa, and the Koranic schools in Islam in the case of Hussein. Their life's work was

---

[51] Robert F. Sayre, *The Examined Self: Benjamin Franklin, Henry Adams, Henry James* (Princeton: Princeton University Press, 1964).

a struggle to impose academic reason over religious voluntarism and theological impositions.

This group of autobiographical historians also share a reformist rather than
revolutionary mood. The in-depth study of the problems through history led
them to realistic positions, avoiding any utopianism that might undermine the
effectiveness of the diagnoses issued to solve these difficulties. All of them also
have in common their autodidacticism, which they share with their Western
counterparts Vico, Gibbon and Adams. They are suspicious of formal and
conventional teaching, which they claim has brought them nothing special in
their journey of knowledge.

Finally, none of them were professionals in history, but all of them were
convinced of the historical tool as an agent of modernisation – and all were
authors of influential historical works. They recognised the performative value
of autobiography, as they intended to develop these values through their first-
person narration.

Fukuzawa Yukichi's Japanese Autobiography (1899)

After all, the present is the result of the past.[52]

Fukuzawa Yukichi published his autobiography in 1899, when he was sixty-
four. His memoir is a personal portrait of Japan in the second half of the
nineteenth century, written by a multifaceted and influential character:
educator, philosopher, writer, reformer and businessman. He was not
a professional historian but an intellectual with Samurai blood who was
persuaded that analysis of the past was an essential tool for preserving
Japan's sacred traditions without closing it off from a modernisation that
he himself promoted in the Meiji era (1868–1912). He used his dual
personality as a contemplative intellectual and cultural promoter to intervene in public debate, founding Keio University and the *Jiji-Shinpō* newspaper. His life was marked by his stern upbringing in the noble Samurai
family of his ancestors, insatiable intellectual curiosity, unbribable moral
character and deep sense of social reform. Although he had no special
public presence and held no great public office, his celebrity and prestige
were so great that he is considered in his country one of the founding figures
of modern Japan.

Fukuzawa was born in Nakatsu (Ōita) in 1835 and died in Tokyo in 1901. In
his childhood, he knew a society based on 'the feudal system with the rigid law
of inheritance: sons of high officials following their father in office, sons of

---

[52] Fukuzawa Yukichi, *The Autobiography of Fukuzawa* (New York: Columbia University Press,
2007), 335.

foot-soldiers always becoming foot-soldiers, and those of the families in between having the same lot for centuries without change'.[53] His father, an artisan who died when Fukuzawa was a year and a half old, wanted him to become a priest. But he eventually decided to devote his life to study and writing. But the beginnings were far from easy. In fact, he attributed his success in study to a lack of certainty about the future: 'Most of us were then actually putting all our energy into our studies without any definite assurance of the future. Yet this lack of future hope was indeed fortunate for us, for it made us better students.'[54]

His teacher Shōzan Shiraishi introduced him to the culture and spirituality preached by Confucius. This traditional influence was supplemented by the Western-style teachings he received, from the age of fourteen, at the Dutch Rangaku school. In 1859 he was commissioned on his first diplomatic mission in America and Europe, an activity he would carry out throughout his life and which was the basis of his multidisciplinary training and writing. This visit, well described in his autobiography, marked a turning point in his life and thought, since he was confirmed in the idea that Japanese reforms were compatible with a certain degree of westernisation of the country. This would counteract the chronic stagnation he observed in the great neighbouring civilisations of China and India.

On his return to Japan, Fukuzawa found the country at the height of the anti-foreign movement. He tells the dramatic story of some neighbours pestering his mother with the false news that he had died while he was travelling. He never knew whether they wanted to torment her or simply have fun at her expense, but he attributed it to xenophobic feeling: 'in the full swing of the anti-foreign sentiment, there was nothing we could do but to keep quiet'.[55] Following his maxim that 'troubled times are best for doing big things',[56] he then considered what he could do to alleviate this feeling. The information gathered during trips to America and Europe resulted in his celebrated and voluminous work _Seiyō Jijō_ ('Western Things'), and earned him renown as an intellectual in his country, where he came to be regarded as the foremost expert on Western civilisation. This led him to conclude that his mission in life was to educate his countrymen in new ways of thinking, precisely to enable Japan to resist European imperialism. The son of the old Samurai was in a position to overcome that old world because he knew it inside out.

Fukuzawa's ideas about individual strength and knowledge of Western political theory were decisive in motivating the Japanese people to embrace

---

[53] Fukuzawa, _Autobiography_, 6. [54] Fukuzawa, _Autobiography_, 92.
[55] Fukuzawa, _Autobiography_, 125. [56] Fukuzawa, _Autobiography_, 187.

modernisation. He never accepted a civil service position that would have provided him with the desired professional and economic stability, but would have prevented him from reflection and study. Particularly illuminating are his reflections on education in his autobiography, on how East and West can complement each other – and, above all, the realism of feeling overtaken by the latter:

> From my own observations in both Occidental and Oriental civilizations, I find that each has certain strong points and weak points bound up in its moral teachings and scientific theories. [. . .] In the education of the East, so often saturated with Confucian teaching, I find two things lacking; that is to say, a lack of studies in number and reason in material culture, and a lack of the idea of independence in spiritual culture. [. . .] Japan could not assert herself among the great nations of the world without full recognition and practice of these two principles. And I reasoned that Chinese philosophy as the root of education was responsible of our obvious shortcomings.[57]

Fukuzawa proves to be a loyal man, embodying many of the qualities one might assign to his peculiar blend of traditional Samurai and modern Japanese culture. When he set up his newspaper, he advised reporters to be vigilant – 'they must limit their statements to what they would be willing to say to the victim face to face'.[58] In addition, he decided that he should not die leaving any debt behind him. At the end of his autobiography, he cannot hide his optimism about what he has achieved in life:

> To my delight Japan was opened to the world. [. . .] I must take advantage of the moment to bring in more of Western civilizations and revolutionize our people's ideas from the roots. Then perhaps it would not be impossible to form a great nation in this far Orient, which would stand counter to Great Britain of the West, and take an active part in the progress of the whole world.[59]

However, he was not content with what he had done, and set himself three goals for the rest of his life that reflect well the magnitude of his personality: first, 'elevating the moral standards of the men and women of my land to make them truly worthy of a civilized nation'; second, 'to encourage a religion – Buddhism or Christianity – to give peaceful influence on a large number of our people'; and third, 'to have a large foundation created for the study of higher sciences in both physical and metaphysical fields'.[60]

Fukuzawa's mind ranged from high ideals to immediate purpose. When he died on 3 February 1901, he was mourned by the whole nation. The emperor sent a special messenger to his family, and the nation's Diet passed an

---

[57] Fukuzawa, *Autobiography*, 214–215.   [58] Fukuzawa, *Autobiography*, 323.
[59] Fukuzawa, *The Autobiography*, 334.   [60] Fukuzawa, *The Autobiography*, 336.

unprecedented resolution of condolence. Proof of his celebrity and recognition is that his figure appears on the current 10,000 Japanese yen banknote. His autobiography is an excellent testimony of a life dedicated to the noble task of improving one's own society through an in-depth study of its problems, especially through its past. He demonstrates, among so many other examples that this Element aims to disseminate, that the autobiographies of historians have both a heuristic and a practical value that it would be a shame to let slip away.

Taha Hussein's Islamic Autobiography (1929)

The sheikh could recite the Quran
and the mother make supplications as much they liked.
The strange thing was that no one in all this company of people
thought about the doctor.[61]

In the midst of her little sister's groans of unbearable pain, everyone was praying and crying around her, but no one thought to call the doctor. This was the challenge Taha Hussein had to face throughout his life: how to reconcile people's natural tendencies to live their religion and appreciate their traditions with the urgency of modernisation?

The parallels between Taha Hussein and Fukuzawa are striking, as they both share the hybrid character of intellectuals and activists, and fought efficiently for the modernisation of their country in the midst of terrible adversity. Born half a century after Fukuzawa, Hussein was one of the founding heroes of the Arab Modernist and Renaissance movement. He was nominated for the Nobel Prize for Literature and has been considered the doyen of Arabic literature. His three autobiographies, gathered under the title *The Days*, are a rich testimony of a blind intellectual who recounts his painful but idealised childhood in a poor rural context, the disease that led to his blindness, a youth cut short by the voluntarism of the teachers at the Al-Azhar Koranic school (later made into a university) and a maturity crowned by a brilliant presence in public life as a doctor of La Sorbonne, a famous writer and a Minister of Education.

Hussein was born in 1889 in Izbet el Kilo, a village in central Upper Egypt in a humble and crowded family: he was the seventh of thirteen children. When he was two, he contracted ophthalmia and, as a result of improper treatment as he dramatically recounts in his autobiography, he became blind. This marked his life, logically, but far from being discouraged, it made him grow up in the face of the

---

[61] Taha Hussein, *The Days: Taha Hussein: His Autobiography in Three Parts* (Cairo: The American University in Cairo Press, 1997), 72.

material adversities, human pettiness and intellectual mediocrity that surrounded him all his life.

When he was still a child, his father sent him to Cairo to attend the primary school (the *kuttab*, the typical elementary school in the Muslim world). Later, he was sent to study religion and Arabic literature at the Al-Azhar school. In his autobiographies he recounts in detail and with regret the retrograde, traditionalist, voluntarist and doctrinaire atmosphere he encountered there, and against which he decided to fight all his life. After completing his studies at the age of eighteen, he decided to continue his studies, and, despite his blindness, he was admitted to the secular Cairo University, which had been founded shortly before.

From then on, it was time for him to decide for himself. Confirming the bond that usually emerges between the author and his subject of study, he decided to undertake a doctoral thesis on sceptical philosopher of the classic period Abu al-'Ala' al-Ma'arri (known as Abulola Moarrensis, 973–1057), also blind like himself. Al-Ma'arri had a reputation as a pessimist, sceptic and atheist, for his tireless fight against superstition and dogmatism. After completing his doctoral studies, convinced of his worth, and persuaded that study was the best antidote to the voluntarist positions he had suffered so much from in his childhood and adolescence, he decided to move to Europe to continue his studies. He moved to the University of Montpellier, where he studied literature, history, French and Latin. He continued his studies at the Sorbonne, where he received a second doctorate, this time for his dissertation on the Tunisian historian and sociologist Ibn Khaldun, analysed in this Element (Section 2).

In 1919, at the age of thirty, Hussein returned to Egypt and was appointed Professor of History and Literature at Cairo University. In *On Pre-Islamic Poetry* (1926), he emerged as a critical intellectual, willing to revise Egypt's cultural and religious tradition from its foundations, not content with assumed truths. In this case, he argued the falsity of some pre-Islamic poetic sources, which some attributed to their scepticism about the reliability of the Qur'an as a valid historical source. He was accused of treating Islam disrespectfully by some theological scholars of Al-Azhar. Although he dodged prison, he had to give up his position in Cairo University in 1931.

Meanwhile, Egypt was evolving towards modernisation, which eventually allowed for his public rehabilitation. In 1950, he was appointed Minister of Education. From this solid public platform, he could apply the ideas that appear in his first two autobiographies: he promoted free education, transformed Koranic schools into conventional primary schools and upgraded several secondary schools into colleges.

His first autobiography (*An Egyptian Childhood*, 1929) was dictated in nine days to his relatives during a holiday in France. It is about his childhood and early years in Koranic school, where he suffered greatly from the intolerance of his teachers. The second volume (*The Stream of Days*, 1940) focuses on his university years, when he could develop his ideas and personality more freely, despite the difficulties of his environment. The third volume (*A Passage to France*, 1967), published decades later, is a more dispassionate and reflective account, with more ideas than stories, more reflections than narrations. These autobiographies are written in the third person, following the well-established tradition among historians' autobiographies that we have seen with Caesar, Vico and Adams. Significantly, however, the third volume shifts to the first person.

In these expressive autobiographies we meet a character seeking to modernise his own Egyptian society and Arab civilisation in general, at a time of tectonic clash between the tradition and modernisation, ruralisation and urbanisation, rationalism and mysticism, Arabisation and westernisation, Islamisation and Christianisation. His motto was:

> not innovation but renovation, the revitalization of a great cultural heritage by bringing the best modes of Western thinking to bear upon it, and this in emulation of forefathers who, in the heyday of Islam, had drawn freely on the resources of Geek civilization.[62]

Because he was blind, all his autobiographies have a dictation-like flavour. The story is a drama, as from the very first pages the author's visual limitations that are not made explicit until late in the book become apparent. Hussein is an intellectual whose blindness has accentuated his auditory capacity and sensitivity to the maximum. Yet, despite the drama of his disability, he never fell into victimhood, despair or fatalism and always felt loved, finding his place in the family and in his neighbourhood. However, the tragedy of the death of his little sister, aged four, and his older brother, who was about to go to medical school, changed everything forever. In the midst of these difficulties, 'nobody remembered to call the doctor'.[63] That stuck with him: it was the same religious blindness – mixed with idleness – that had caused his own physical blindness. From then on, he swore to himself that he could be true to his religion without having to give up the advances that science and technology had brought. That was the attitude with which he approached his early religious studies at the Al-Azhar – the Islamic religious institution that would later become a university.

What makes Hussain's autobiography so valuable is its extraordinary expressiveness, the fruit of its oral origin. The descriptions of the characters are anthological: the authoritarian teacher, the wayward student, the kind but distant

---

[62] Hussein, *The Days*, 5.   [63] Hussein, *The Days*, 72.

brother. Nothing escapes his literary gaze, framed by an extraordinary sensitivity born of a fine ear – and intensified by his lack of vision. In the first autobiography – the most brilliant of the three – the narrative becomes increasingly dramatic until the final pages, where he recounts the inquisitorial process to which he was subjected, along with two other students, for defying the established conventions of the Al-Azhar: the impossibility of dissent in academic matters and an invincible tendency of most professors to bypass the cognitive and rational process, always appealing to arguments from authority.

Few literary writings have offered so much to improve the world. Taha Hussein proved with his life and his writings that difficulties can be overcome with tenacity, steadfastness, courage and a touch of providential luck.

Gu Jiegang's Chinese Autobiography (1931)

Scholarship does not consist in blind acceptance,
but in genuine research.[64]

Gu Jiegang was one of the most influential Chinese historians in the twentieth century. He was born in 1893 in the era of the Sino-Japanese confrontation and China's modernisation crisis. Since his adolescence, he has had an inner tension between critical analysis of historical processes and activism to solve them. The latter led him to join the Socialist Party during the 1911 Revolution in China. But he soon became disillusioned as so many Western European intellectuals committed to the Communist Party: 'I gradually perceived that the members [of the Socialist Party] were not what they should be.'[65] He then became a reformist rather than a revolutionary, an attitude that was to inform all his intellectual activity for the rest of his life – and assimilates it to the mood of the other three historians included in this section. As a student at Peking University, he developed a reflexive rather than an activist interest and, like Fukuzawa in Japan and Hussein in Egypt, he decided to use a new historical narrative to contribute to China's modernisation. From that moment, he fought to introduce a critical attitude to the analysis of historical and literary sources, however sacred they might appear. Its strategy consisted of producing major historical works like his monumental *Debates on Ancient History*, and promoting a scholar-civic movement known as *Doubting Antiquity School*.

Gu published his autobiography in 1931, when he was barely thirty-three years old. As in Fukuzawa and Hussein, this text is an expressive platform for understanding the tensions between tradition and modernity in Chinese culture

---

[64] Jiegang Gu, *The Autobiography of a Chinese Historian* (Leiden: Brill, 1931), 161.
[65] Gu, *Autobiography*, 29.

during the first half of the twentieth century. Like Vico and the twentieth-century French ego-historians, the first impulse to write his autobiography came not from within, but from a request to write a preface for a symposium on Chinese history. What was to be a brief and conventional academic text became a dense intellectual ego-history of 180 pages. He takes advantage of the request to write a preface to examine his own historiographical production:

> I wanted to seize this opportunity to clarify the methods I employ in my study of ancient history, and the steps by which I have arrived at my conclusions. Since one fact cannot stand by itself, I was compelled, in order to make clear the connection, to discuss innumerable other facts along with it. Whether or not the result corresponds to what is ordinarily considered a preface is really of little consequence.'[66]

Consistent with E. H. Carr's precept decades later in *What Is History?* to 'study the historian before studying the history' (as mentioned in the introduction to this Element), Gu enjoyed reading the prefaces or postscripts of history books in which some biographical details of the author appear. This gives him one of the keys to the function of his own autobiography, and of historians' autobiographies in general: 'It helps one to understand better the origin of the work and the derivation of the ideas which are thus placed in their proper historical setting.'[67]

In both his academic work and his autobiography, Gu delved into the origins of Chinese civilisation, particularly the *Five Classics*, one of the key texts of the traditional Confucianist canon, to test the authenticity of a background that took the form of a founding myth. He was co-founder and leader of the *Doubting Antiquity School*, which advocated a demystification of China's ancient past through rational and scientific literary criticism. However, he is much more respectful of his religious (Confucian) tradition than Fukuzawa is of the Japanese or Taha Hussein of the Arab-Islamic one. A comparison between these three autobiographies gives an idea of why Japan achieved greater modernisation and westernisation shortly after Fukuzawa's time, while China an Egypt were more reluctant at Hussein's and Gu's time, because the resistance of society and the repressions of the middle twentieth-century rulers were much greater.

In his autobiography, Gu argues that a demystified study of China's glorious and mythologised past would lead to a more modernised and rationalised vision of the future. His leitmotiv and passion was 'how to reconcile the concept of a golden age in antiquity with the ideal of a developing society'.[68] To this end, he began his study of the past from an essentialist and theoretical perspective, but was soon captivated by an inductive and historicist one: 'But it was not until later that I realized that was the historical element in the classics that really

---

[66] Gu, *Autobiography*, 184.   [67] Gu, *Autobiography*, 5.   [68] Gu, *Autobiography*, 14–15.

attracted me.'[69] Compatible with his radical heuristic critique of tradition ('such stories [on the origins of China] had no basis in fact and were after all only traditions'[70]), he was convinced that China's *real* past provided radical sources of inspiration both for challenging old mythical traditions and creating and authorising new ones. He sought to abolish the idea of an immutable Chinese essence existing from time immemorial and was therefore sceptical that Chinese history was simply the history of Confucianism.

Gu ends his account around 1915, when he was barely thirty years old. He would spent the rest of his life studying as an autodidact, like so many of the historians included in this Element, not least Vico, Gibbon and Adams: 'I obtained next to nothing from the classes that I attended.'[71] Later, when the Cultural Revolution broke out in 1966, he suffered a torment typical of some intellectuals who had driven the modernisation of their respective countries during the period of late colonisation: stigmatised as reactionary, he suffered public humiliation and was purged in Maoist China. In the early 1970s, he was released and spent the last decade of his life in well-deserved serenity. As he describes himself in his autobiography, he was a man 'who combines in himself a love of the scientific method, a sceptical attitude toward the past, a settled purpose, inflexible courage, and a mind filled with unsolved problems'.[72]

Gu did not achieve the celebrity of the other three historian-autobiographers included in this section. Moreover, he wrote his autobiography when he was still very young, thus depriving us of access to his attitude towards the great historical events unleashed by the Communist revolution in China. Yet his testimony is an invaluable ego-document in a tradition like China's, where autobiographies of intellectuals and public figures are rare.

Nirad C. Chaudhuri's Indian Autobiography (1951)

The product of study is not the book but the man.[73]

Nirad C. Chaudhuri's autobiography is the best example of the making of a historian through autobiography rather than the making of an autobiography through the historian, and confirms the privilege of enjoying such works. He was unknown, in India or abroad, until he unexpectedly came to fame with the publication of his autobiography in 1951. At that time, he was fifty-four years old and looking more towards retirement than a new life as a writer.

---

[69] Gu, *Autobiography*, 23–24.   [70] Gu, *Autobiography*, 31.   [71] Gu, *Autobiography*, 162.
[72] Gu, *Autobiography*, 182.
[73] Nirad C. Chaudhuri, *The Autobiography of an Unknown Indian* (New York: New York Review Books, 1951), 342.

Chaudhuri's *Autobiography of an Unknown Indian* is an impressive narrative from imperial idealised noon to postcolonial turmoiled India. It describes civilisations that no longer exist, having succumbed to the intense encounter between ancestral Hindu traditions and British imperial modernisation. Some years after its publication, he recounted some details of his first autobiographical impulse:

> It came in this manner. As I lay awake on in the night of May 4–5, 1947, an idea suddenly flashed into my mind. Why, instead of merely regretting the work of history you cannot write, I asked myself, do you not write the history you have passed through and seen enacted before your eyes, and which would not call for research? The answer too was instantaneous: I will. I also decided to give it the form of an autobiography. Quietened by this decision I fell asleep. Fortunately, this idea was not mollified by the deplorable lack of energy which was habitual with me. The very next morning I sat down to my typewriter and drafted a few paragraphs.[74]

It took him nine months to complete his vivid autobiography. The book was finished by the spring of 1949 and was acclaimed by academic and media critics from the beginning. Its parallelisms with Eire's autobiography, analysed in Section 6, are amazing: the same eagerness to tell the story of his childhood, the same fervour to denounce authoritarian tendencies, and the same public recognition and sales success.

Chaudhuri was born in 1897, in Kishoregunj in East Bengal, then under British rule and later made independent as Bangladesh in 1971. He was the second of eight children of liberal upper-caste Hindu parents. The family tradition was attached to Brahmoism, a religious monotheistic and social reformist movement emerged during the Bengal Renaissance, the original Indian independence movement. The narration begins his growing up in the idealised Victorian society of imperial Bengal, which came crashing down in 1947 with the fall of the British Empire. He candidly describes the peaceful villages of his rural Bengali childhood (Kishoreganj, Bangram and Kalikutch), and his youth in Calcutta.

However, by 1905, radical nationalist ideas began to dominate Bengali public life. Amid the turmoil, he opposed the nationalism and anti-colonialism that rapidly took hold in India. These tendencies seemed to him childish and adolescent reactions of those who break away from parental security and indulge in an excess of autonomy, which in fact leads to utopian attitudes. He tried to position himself as a moderate, always eschewing the victimhood or exclusivism of some of these extreme political options.

---

[74] Chaudhuri, *Autobiography*, 10–11.

However, he soon realised with sorrow that 'in demagogic politics the less extreme never has any chance against the more extreme'.[75] This is an essential rule in any civil war process. The major problem he detected lay in the divorce between the unreflective activists whose idealism drives them to engage in politics and the well-educated intellectuals whose pragmatism leads them to turn away from it:

> The brighter boys, going in naturally for the coveted prizes of Indian life like government service, or as the second best for the professions, drifted towards leading purely private lives, because they dared not spoil their worldly prospects by participation in public affairs frowned upon by the government, or, if they themselves dared, their parents dragged them back. On the other hand, with rare exceptions, political activity and agitation became the business of an insufficiently educated, insufficiently intelligent, and insufficiently cultured, though serious and earnest-minded, class, and this gradually brought down the standard of political life till it seemed to have become the monopoly of pig-headed fools or faddists. The Indian middle class became separated into two distinct wings.[76]

Although he was not a professional historian, in the chapter 'Initiation to Scholarship', he recognises that he 'felt irresistibly attracted by the history and methodology of every branch of learning'.[77] Eventually, he consolidated the habit of 'thinking historically',[78] which even led him to explain Europe's decline by its loss of memory: 'I cannot understand how the European man, after having attained the high degree of historical consciousness which he did in the nineteenth century, can have stepped back from it to the uncultured man's bondage to the present and the still more uncultured man's bondage to the eschatology of political dogma. [. . .] I ask myself: Are we witnessing a whole society's senile decay of memory?'[79] No one can deny that this diagnosis is still fully valid.

Chaudhuri's autobiographical impulse came from this preoccupation, since he conceives his account as an exercise in descriptive ethnology rather than properly autobiography, 'more of a national than personal history',[80] as a historical text rather than a memoir:

> The story I want to tell is the story of the struggle of a civilization with a hostile environment, in which the destiny of British rule in India became necessarily involved. My main intention is thus historical, and since I have written the account with the utmost honesty and accuracy of which I am capable, the intention in my mind has become mingled with the aspiration that the book may be regarded as a contribution to contemporary history.[81]

---

[75] Chaudhuri, *Autobiography*, 237.   [76] Chaudhuri, *Autobiography*, 261–262.
[77] Chaudhuri, *Autobiography*, 343.   [78] Chaudhuri, *Autobiography*, 353.
[79] Chaudhuri, *Autobiography*, 354.   [80] Chaudhuri, *Autobiography*, 483.
[81] Chaudhuri, *Autobiography*, xix.

If Europe's decline has been due to forgetting its own tradition, argued Chaudhuri, so has that of India and Bengal. From 1921 onwards, he never ceased to experience a painful sense of decadence: 'during these years everything about us was decaying, literally everything ranging from our spiritual and moral ideals to our material culture, and nothing really live or organic arose to take their place. I have never even read about such a process as I have passed through: it was unadulterated decadence'.[82] As a consequence, the end of his autobiography is one of the saddest I have ever read: by 1921, his 'low spirits were absolute. There seemed to be no cure for them'.[83]

However, we know from his biography that he pulled through and became a highly respected writer both in India and in England: after the publication of his autobiography, he never gave up writing, usually based on experiences gained on his travels from a historical perspective. In 1955, he travelled abroad for the first time, and wrote *A Passage to England* (1959) of his experiences in England, Paris and Rome. In 1987, he published the sequel of his autobiography, *Thy Hand Great Anarch!* He kept writing until the age of ninety-nine. He died in Oxford, two years later, in 1999.

Autobiography of an Unknown Indian is at once a literary, autobiographical and historiographical narrative: it is difficult to find a more penetrating account of the ancient Indian mentality combined with the brief but profound British Western imprint. In narrative terms, it is the autobiography I have enjoyed most in the preparation of this Element, alongside his kindred spirit Carlos Eire, and those by Steedman, Conway and Lerner. The following section is devoted to these three brave female autobiographical voices.

5 Gender Perspectives
Carolyn Steedman, Jill Ker Conway, Gerda Lerner

The autobiographies of Carolyn Steedman, Jill Ker Conway and Gerda Lerner analysed in this section, and those of others of their generation such as Natalie Zemon Davis, Gabrielle M. Spiegel, Luisa Passerini, Élisabeth Roudinesco and Sheila Fitzpatrick, lead this genre to its highest quotas of literary quality, human sensitivity and historiographical value.[84] Their reading should be part of the conventional training of any student of history since they provide us with stories

---

[82] Chaudhuri, *Autobiography*, 378.   [83] Chaudhuri, *Autobiography*, 482.

[84] Luisa Passerini, *Autobiography of a Generation* (Hanover: Wesleyan University Press, 1996); Elisabeth Roudinesco, *Généalogies* (Paris: Fayard, 1994); Sheila Fitzpatrick, *My Father's Daughter: Memories of an Australian Childhood* (Carlton: Melbourne University Press, 2010); Jaume Aurell, 'Performative Academic Careers: Gabrielle Spiegel and Natalie Davis', *Rethinking History* 13.1 (2009): 53–64.

that perfectly combine the various facets of existence, from the most vital to the most profoundly intellectual and specifically historiographical.

In addition, their performative and polyphonic voices promote the emergence of the racial, ethnic, class or gender concerns relevant to representing identity today. These women historians deploy autobiography to explore aspects of their identity and to understand or even construct the self in the act of writing. This is particularly evident in the case of the autobiographies by women or minorities, who have often fought hard to equal their white male colleagues' academic success, a particularly harsh battle in the case of Conway and Lerner. Indeed, their autobiographical essays are currently at the vanguard of innovation among historians' autobiographies.

The increasingly prevalent female autobiographical voice among historians is linked with the progressive incorporation of women into academia after the 1960s. After decades of a growing, but still, marginal influence, many women became established in the discipline in the 1980s and 1990s, particularly in North America (Canada and the United States), notably Gabrielle M. Spiegel, Carolyn Steedman, Joan Scott, Natalie Davis, Nancy Partner and Lynn Hunt, but also in Europe, notably Janet Nelson, Averil Cameron and Catherine Coquery-Vidrovitch, and in India, notably Romila Thapar, among many others. It was not strange, therefore, that some of them should choose to write stories about some of their experiences. Reading with gender and scholarship in mind has much to teach us as readers. Helen Buss has explained that,

> For these human subjects, their lives as writers and intellectuals and as women in the academy have problematized a multiplicity of often painfully conflicted identities, which, ironically, make them seek the academic life as a place where they can accommodate this multiplicity. Their texts are attempts to bring the intellectual process of critical thinking to bear on their own various self-identities and to hold these in balance without oppressing any aspect of what or who has made them. The relationship of life and academy is inevitably fraught with the ambivalence that many of these women feel as the result of perceiving themselves as subjects from the margins.[85]

The autobiographies of Steedman, Conway and Lerner, the texts selected for this section, tend to approach the genre as an experiment with narrative. Gerda Lerner declares that everything in her story is true because she has tried to support memory with historical research and evidence, but she feels that writing an autobiography is different from just collecting surviving data. Rather, it is looking inside to sort out the clutter, to discern enough to make a pattern, to find a meaning beyond the event that extends to others: something that says not only

---

[85] Helen M. Buss, *Repossessing the World: Reading Memoirs by Contemporary Women* (Waterloo: Wilfrid Laurier University Press, 2002), 169–170.

'this happened to me', but also 'this is the meaning of what happened to me'. This process concludes with the narrative of one's own life –finite, and inevitably subjective and biased: 'One keeps reordering the past in the light of one's current insights and so what one sets down are not the facts, but a story. An explanatory myth at worst, an entertaining tale at best.'[86]

This group of autobiographies shows the full narrative and historiographical potential of historians' memoirs. They are models of interventional autobiography in that they use the first-person narrative as a way of intervening in debates within the discipline. Steedman adds to the charm of Conway's and Lerner's autobiographies a considerable theoretical and epistemological nuance. She would be to Vico what Conway and Lerner are to Gibbon and Adams: the former challenge previously established intellectual categories, while the latter present autobiographical accounts that integrate all facets of life.

These narratives show the full potential of autobiography, turning it into an artefact of both disciplinary and rhetorical experimentation. They practise it as a way of expressing new realities – or the same historical realities but from other points of view, itself a postmodern move. As Steedman argues in the introduction to her autobiography,

> So virtually the only prose narratives which are accorded the suspension of disbelief today are the autobiographers' attempts to narrate the history of a real life or the biographers' carefully documented historical reconstructions of lives in times past. Even this concession is not made by readers influenced by postmodern criticism, which calls into question the possibility of apprehending reality from a single point of view. Hence the convention in many forms of modern narrative of switching points of view, and leaving open the possibility of many endings for the story.[87]

They thus use autobiographical narrative *virtually* in the same experimental way that Picasso used dicentric cubism to narrate the horrors of the Spanish Civil War in his *Guernica*.

Carolyn Steedman's Psychoanalytical Autobiography (1986)

The perspective of the dream must have shifted several times.[88]

Carolyn Steedman's autobiography marks a turning point in the autobiographies of historians: its experimental character, its intelligent use of memory, its polyphonic

---

[86] Gerda Lerner, *Fireweed: A Political Autobiography* (Philadelphia: Temple University Press, 2003), 1.

[87] Carolyn Steedman, *Landscape for a Good Woman: A Story of Two Lives* (New Brunswick: Rutgers University Press, 1986), 5.

[88] Steedman, *Landscape*, 28.

authorial voice, its diverse sources and its interaction with various disciplines make it an inescapable milestone in autobiographical literature conceived as a way of understanding how the historical discipline and writing function. There is a mysterious, but real, connection between Steedman's and Vico's autobiographies, involving scientific inquiry through the (almost psychoanalytic but definitely epistemological) analysis of one's own life.

Steedman was born in 1947 and grew up in South London in a working-class family environment. She studied history at Sussex at a time when it was at the cutting edge of innovation, and worked as a primary school teacher between 1974 and 1981. She published her autobiography of childhood when she was thirty-nine. It deals with her working-class experience and she challenges conventional accounts and established genres. Her introspective analysis combines feminist, Marxist and psychoanalytic perspectives, blends autobiography with academic and fictional writing, and provides an alternative to traditional historical narratives and methodology – and, more specifically, to the traditional narratives of mother–daughter romances. Deconstructing sexism in favour of gender categories and applying the social history methods to her own story, she constructs a bridge between social class and sexual identity. By examining her own life using her academic knowledge, she challenges the conventional tendency of 1980s historians and sociologists to collective and generalised psycho-Freudian analysis.

The permanent paradox of this Element, and perhaps what makes it relevant, is the continuing dialogue between personal memories and academic discourse. Steedman is the first professional historian – albeit with a typical indirect route of the scholars of this generation, like his Warwick predecessor E.P. Thompson – to be discussed in this Element, but at the same time she is able to transcend the formalism and neglect of the audience to which some professional scholars tend. The Element's polyphonic nature requires the use of multiple sources, which Steedman deploys flexibly: her personal recollections, her childhood and adult readings – both academic and fictional. She is devoted to clarifying the difference between official or professional history and the other kinds of stories we imagine, dream and tell. Yet, crucially, she uses autobiography not for an aesthetic, narcissistic or therapeutic purpose, but rather for epistemological and interpretative ones. The result is an unconventional, multi-layered and insightful text in which the author deals with issues such as social recognition and conventions, social identity and class, the psychology of family relationships, the relationship between mothers and daughters, the various manifestations of patriarchy and matriarchy, forms of desire, norms of social inclusion and exclusion – and, crucially, class and gender consciousness.

And Steedman does so through childhood autobiography, a subgenre that is always fertile in her imagination, as we also found with Hussein's autobiography and will find in Eire's autobiography (Section 6). She increases *Landscape*'s historiographic interest with its strong psychoanalytical component, too. The whole plot revolves around the unravelling of a dream she had when she was three and which she describes at the beginning of the book: 'A woman hurried along, having crossed from the houses behind. [. . .] Several times she turned and came some way back towards me, admonishing, shaking her finger. [. . .] I wish I knew what she was doing, and what she wanted me to do.'[89]

Steedman's use of a dream for the beginning of her narrative is, of course, a familiar literary strategy. It locates her narrative at the crossroad of memory, imagination and history, heightening the sense of childhood fragility, lack of awareness, and dependence on adults. It alerts the reader to the prominent presence of a female character in her story, the imposing figure of her mother. Yet it also allows the reader to empathise with Steedman's idea of the relevance – but also the relativity – of the stories we tell: 'The perspective of the dream must have shifted several times.' As she describes her childhood, Steedman slowly unravels the meaning of the dream, which has become an element of the past lying at the heart of her present: 'it is my interpretative device, the means by which I can tell a story' – the story of her childhood.[90]

Steedman interprets her childhood feelings of exclusion by blending personal memory with academic information she learned from the working-class women's autobiographies she read in her twenties and the academic bibliography she studied in her thirties. Her autobiography reveals imagination in content, heterodoxy in form, and lack of restrictions in method. She eschews linear narrative, moving back and forth between her personal histories. Trained in the most conventional British social history tradition, she finds new ways to narrate history beyond the forms of grand theory and narrative, and the types of determinism that would otherwise have fixed available meanings into place. She assembles a case history, taking her information from 'the bits and pieces from which psychological selfhood is made'.[91] She shows how autobiography might become a historical-historiographical instrument to explain marginalised aspects of the past, or at least approach them from a different perspective, since sometimes scientific knowledge is not enough:

> Personal interpretations of past time – the stories that people tell themselves in order to explain how they got to the place they currently inhabit – are often in deep and ambiguous conflict with the official interpretative devices of a culture.

---

[89] Steedman, *Landscape*, 27–28.   [90] Steedman, *Landscape*, 28.
[91] Steedman, *Landscape*, 7.

This book is organized around a conflict like this, taking as a starting point the structures of class analysis and schools of cultural criticism that cannot deal with everything there is to say about my mother's life.[92]

Steedman experiments with her autobiographical account to create a connection between the ideas expressed in singular stories with the general tenets held by scholars of history, sociology and psychology, and to challenge them. This allows her to demystify, in an academically sophisticated way but at the same time with the effectiveness of an autobiographical narrative, some of the most established ideas about women in society.

In the end, Steedman believes that she has really written history – although another kind of history. As she admitted in a meta-autobiographical exercise some years later, 'It is for the potentialities of that community offered by historical consciousness, I suppose, that I want what I have written to be called history, and not autobiography.'[93] Nevertheless, it is a form of history different from what professional historians have already done, since she did not do any real empirical research for the book and check marriage registers, census returns or hospital records. Instead, she wanted to write about 'the stories we make for ourselves, and the social specificity of our understanding of those stories'.[94] She thus seeks an understanding of stories rather than their historicity: the way we recall, refigure and interpret them.

Landscape for a Good Woman is an extraordinary academic work that loses none of its autobiographical value. Steedman realised that first-person narrative gives historians the opportunity to place themselves noticeably into their own critical writing, as some of the key contributors to certain subdisciplines, such as Carolyn Steedman, Geoff Eley and Natalie Davis (social history), Gabrielle M. Spiegel (history of historiography), Dominick LaCapra (intellectual history), and William Sewell (social-linguistic history) have shown with their respective autobiographies.[95] These interventional autobiographies perform their selves and the disciplines they practise as they write their historical-autobiographical texts, turning autobiography into academic criticism, personal scholarship, self-inclusive scholarship, interdisciplinary artefact and cross-genre writing: the personal background is not an incidental fact of research but what shapes the process of searching and discovering.

---

92 Steedman, *Landscape*, 6.
93 Carolyn Steedman, 'History and Autobiography: Different Pasts', in *Steedman, Past Tenses: Essays on Writing, Autobiography and History* (London: Rivers Oram Press, 1992), 41–50, here 50.
94 Steedman, *Landscape*, 5.
95 This is what made me define some of these autobiographies as 'interventional': Jaume Aurell, 'Making History by Contextualizing Oneself: Autobiography as Historiographical Intervention', *History and Theory* 54 (2015): 244–268.

Jill Ker Conway's Academic Autobiography (1994)

I wanted to convey my sense of my education,
of my liberation through access to education,
and of the variety of steps by
which I arrived at taking charge of my own life.[96]

Many of the twentieth-century historians who have written autobiographies have had to deal with apparently monotonous lives and therefore to emphasise the intellectual interest of their lives. This is not the case with Jill Ker Conway. Her real life would be worthy of making into a fictional film. The fast-paced prose of her autobiographical trilogy, moving like the gallop of a thoroughbred horse, is undoubtedly a match for her dramatic life. *The Road from Coorain* (1989) tells the story of her childhood and youth until her move to the United States in 1960. It became an international bestseller and was made into a TV movie in 2001. Her second autobiography, *True North* (1994) – my personal favourite – opens with her flight-trip to Boston at the age of 18 and covers the period up to her acceptance of the presidency of Smith College. It is the most academically oriented of her autobiographies. *A Woman's Education* (2001), more conceptual than the two earlier texts, recounts her experiences as president of Smith College and her thoughts on women's experiences and aspirations, and the form that higher education for women should take.

Conway was born in Hillston, New South Wales, Australia, in 1934 and raised in a family farm, Coorain, in the middle of nowhere. She did not attend the school, since she was educated by her mother and a country governess, spending her youth carrying out domestic and farm labours. When she was eleven, his father died in an accident while working on the farm, in circumstances that have never been fully clarified. The family never knew whether it had actually been a suicide, and carried the weight of that doubt with them always. After a drought of almost seven years which doomed the farm, the family (mother, Jill and her two brothers) moved to Sydney. She studied History and English at the University of Sydney until 1958. Resisting strong pressure from her mother not to leave her alone, she decided to move to the United States in 1960, looking for an air of personal autonomy. In a dramatic opening to her True North, she recounts her ambivalent thoughts during the flight to Boston, about the past he was leaving behind and the hopeful future she had ahead. After a period of uncertainty and anxiety, she was accepted into the history programme at Harvard University, where she received her doctorate in 1969. There she met the man who would be her husband until his death: John Conway, a Canadian professor and war hero, but prone to depression.

---

[96] Jill K. Conway, *True North: A Memoir* (New York: Alfred A. Knopf, 1994), 49.

After a decade teaching at the University of Toronto, she moved with him to Boston in 1975 to become the first woman president of Smith College, a position she held until 1985 – the part of her story told in her third autobiography, *A Woman's Education.*

Conway is both an engaging storyteller and an insightful scholar. She offers vivid descriptions of her changing surroundings and provides insights into the psychological process of adapting to each new place. As a child and adolescent, she had to fight hard against a culture that considered the love of learning pretentious and impractical. So, when she arrived at Harvard from her native Australia, she delighted in academic work, the interactions of teachers and students debating questions of freedom, religion, civic responsibility, politics or issues of gender. As one of the few female candidates at the university, she found herself firmly placed in the academic arena, intervening in theoretical and practical debates about the emerging women's movement of the time. She moved to Canada and succeeded in becoming a teacher and administrator at the University of Toronto, though she continually confronted evidence of gender bias. With another relevant female intellectual and brilliant historian, Natalie Zemon Davis, she helped found one of the first women's studies programmes in North America before Conway went off to Smith College and Davis to Berkeley. When telling these academic stories, Conway portrays herself as a 1960s modern woman who works hard at her intellectual and administrative tasks while also serving as hostess and caregiver to her husband. Experience from life and knowledge from academia flow through the text to converge in one illuminating narrative stream. Finally, as university vice president, she worked to redress inequities throughout the school's employment structure, from faculty to janitorial staff.

Private and academic matters merge naturally in the narrative. Her doctoral dissertation on the first generation of American women reformers confirmed her belief that successful women use well-thought-out methods for achieving their goals but that, when they report on their achievements, they often disguise the extent of their drive and planning, perceiving this as socially unacceptable and, therefore, veiling the truth about their work. Thus, Conway uses her autobiography to approach twentieth-century feminism under a new light and from a different perspective – one that privileges women's personal agency instead of subordinating it to others. Parallels with other women historians of her generation, such as Annie Kriegel, Élisabeth Roudinesco, Luisa Passerini, Steedman and Lerner, are obvious, as they also sought to relate the historical subjects they analysed as scholars to their personal experiences, professional aspirations, intellectual options and ideological claims.

Conway rebels against the romantic plot that women have traditionally acted out, agreeing to present themselves as passive players in somebody else's story.

Some years after the publication of *True North*, she recognised that she wrote her autobiographies because she was interested,

> in seeing if I could come up with a life plot that wasn't a romance, because the archetypical life plot for women in Western society is the bourgeois romance. [. . .] But I didn't want to write an odyssey – to just take over the archetypal male plot and create a conquering heroine. I was looking for a way to narrate a life story of a woman that would pay due respect to her attachments to men and to family but would be about something else entirely.[97]

Through her autobiography, Conway defends the conviction that patriarchal conditions and language have so thoroughly stifled women that they have not been able to write with complete authenticity about their own lives. She posits that, when they write their autobiography, women tend to fall back on a more romantic view, using the passive, rather than the active, voice, portraying themselves not as agents but as objects, and focusing on interior life rather than on action. Thus, her authoritative and engaging discussion of agency – claiming an active role in one's own life, fighting against difficulties and setbacks – is the best practical basis for the theoretical foundations of feminism. She conceives agency as the capacity to act on one's own behalf rather than being acted upon, to actively shape one's life experiences. Thus, she concludes, acknowledgement of one's agency is a major step towards full self-realisation.

Conway's allergy to academic jargon illustrates her concern for her audience and the wider possibilities of autobiography. She sought 'a more inclusive rhetoric for feminism today',[98] finding in autobiography not only a scholarly channel for discussion of feminist quarrels, but also a way to react against some polarised feminist beliefs on both sides that she did not share. She combated women's sentimentalism and self-victimisation as she engaged in her memoir, which she described as 'my personal testament in opposition to the sentimental school of thought about women'.[99] Her successor in this book, Gerda Lerner, proved with her life and autobiography that she had learned well the lesson Conway had taught her fellow female historians.

Gerda Lerner's Drama Autobiography (2003)

Acting just as if fireweed could make a forest.[100]

Gerda Lerner's autobiography is a gripping narrative of an epic scholar who experienced an idealised childhood shattered by the drama of war, the harassment of Jewish persecution, the collapse of the outstanding culture of

---

[97] Conway, *True North*, 45.   [98] Conway, *True North*, 48.   [99] Conway, *True North*, 49.
[100] Lerner, *Fireweed*, 373.

fin-de-siècle Vienna, a traumatic emigration to America, and the personal commitment to social causes for which she risked the stability she had begun to experience in her new country. Her story is the narration of an identity lost in adolescence, and the constant struggle to recover it: a family split by the war and which she tries to reunite; a childhood and a citizenship that Hitler stole from her and which she tries to regain in the United States; and, above all, the irrepressible impetus of her desire to be a writer, which governs all of her autobiographical writing.

Lerner's *Fireweed* is a thrilling account of a life of hardship. She was born in Vienna in 1920 to an upper-class family whose members came from various parts of Central Europe (Germany, Hungary, Bohemia and Moravia) and had inherited the cosmopolitan air and cultural sensibility of the *fin-de-siècle* Vienna generation. Her parents complemented each other. Her father was a pharmacist while her bohemian mother enjoyed the sparkling cultural atmosphere of the time: 'If my father's ideal was respectability, my mother's was creativity.'[101] After the *Anschluss* in 1938, her father became involved in the anti-Nazi resistance and had to flee to Liechtenstein and Switzerland. After her father's escape, she was imprisoned for six weeks in terrible conditions. In 1939, she managed to emigrate to the United States assisted by the family of his fiancé Bobby Jensen, in a veritable epic that she recounts in her autobiography. She worked there as a waitress, salesperson, office clerk and X-ray technician, but her real dream was to write fiction and poetry. After breaking up with Jensen, she married Carl Lerner, a theatre director who was a member of the US Communist Party.

The couple fought for a number of causes such as trade unionism, civil rights and anti-militarism. They suffered under the rise of McCarthyism in the 1950s – especially with the Hollywood blacklist, which implicated her husband. When she was in her forties, she enrolled at the New School for Social Research, where she received a bachelor's degree in 1963. Then she continued with graduate studies at Columbia University, earning her PhD there in 1966. At the age of forty-six, she began to dream of fulfilling her vocation as a writer through history: 'My career as historian began almost by accident; I thought of it as a way of acquiring a skill necessary to my writing.'[102] In the 1960s and 1970s, she published some influential scholarly books and articles that helped establish women's history as a recognised field of study: she is now considered one of the founders of the academic field of women's history.

Lerner masters autobiographical writing as brilliantly as her colleagues Steedman and Conway. Her autobiography is not a collection of several disjointed stories of experience, but a coherent account of a life that takes on a unity in the midst of

---

[101] Lerner, *Fireweed*, 59.   [102] Lerner, *Fireweed*, 367.

intense adversity. It reads like a novel, but with the added charm of the real. She is particularly skilful in recounting the most dramatic moments of her life. The climax of the narrative comes when the Gestapo enter and search her flat in Vienna while her father is in Liechtenstein on a business trip, trying to avoid arrest. She is arrested with his mother, and spends some weeks in prison, a time which she 'could not deal with, and even as I am writing this I cannot deal with it'.[103] Lerner demonstrates that autobiography is a particularly appropriate genre for expressing personal traumas that historians do not usually recount in their proper historical narratives, as we have seen in the case of Sima in antiquity and will see in the case of postcolonisation narratives by Bethwell Ogot in Africa, Carlos Eire in Latin America and Wang Gungwu in Southeast Asia. From that moment on, a life of hardship, flight and disappointment in love begins, until she found the love of her life in a passionate but humble Hollywood scriptwriter. Lerner's extraordinary literary-historical skills are best displayed in the narratives of family rifts and disappointments in love. The pain of loss or disenchantment wells up like blood from a deep wound, but in the end the serenity of considered judgement prevails.

Lerner suffers discrimination for being Jewish, for being a woman, for her incorruptible criticism as a committed intellectual, and for her low socioeconomic status in American exile. She even suffers attempted sexual abuse by her mother's boyfriend, which leaves her terrified and forever clouds her relationship with her mother. But she is never shown as a woman of apathy or victimhood, or one defeated by the violent onslaught of her context. On the contrary, she is always looking for a way out that will allow her to move forward. Like the first flowers that appear after a devastating forest fire – *Fireweed* – she always finds the energy to rise from her own ashes. Once rooted, it is very difficult for them to wither again:

> After a forest fire rages over a mountainside, leaving everything black and charred and lifeless, there is a time when life, even the promise of life, seem to have vanished from that desolate landscape. And then, first with green shoots, then red flowers, the fireweed comes out of the barren ground, insisting on survival, pushing its persistent roots under the ashes of destruction. Soon, the black and rocky landscape is punctured by patches of small red growth, which will spread and make solid, make space of hope and future transformation.[104]

Lerner also demonstrates that the vocation of historian is not only compatible with that of writer, but that in her case it acquires its full meaning. She does not need to change rhetorical register as a writer of fictional, true or autobiographical stories. Her authorship gathers them all. The descriptions of her failures as a fiction writer in her early years in the United States are particularly revealing. After rejection by publishers, she returned again and again to her writing, trying

---

[103] Lerner, *Fireweed*, 105.   [104] Lerner, *Fireweed*, 373.

to improve its content and form. The reader, especially if they are a historian, is thus challenged by and identifies with these inner struggles, which move seamlessly between euphoria and depression.

Lerner's whole life is a struggle to fulfil her dream of becoming a writer. She finally does so, but in a somewhat unexpected way, through history. In fact, she decides to interrupt the story of her life when, after all the agonising, she manages to start studying history. She then begins the second part of her life, in which the suffering seems to have vanished, her goals achieved, the discrimination far away and her family enjoying a stability she had been deprived of all her life. But, from her later writings, we know that she never stopped fighting for what she believed to be just, especially in the struggle against the ethnic, class and gender discriminations she had suffered so much. She does not behave as one who sits complacently on the hard-won chair of social and professional recognition. Rather, she tries to bring to fruition all the qualities that have emerged from a life of struggle against inner and outer hardships, by effectively engaging in the struggle against social disadvantage and on behalf of those who suffer discrimination of any kind: 'My work as a women's historian has been noted for taking race and class into consideration.'[105]

Lerner imbues her autobiography with all its noblest meanings. Although it is shown to be a genre with a notably subjective charge, the historian Lerner manages to convey a high degree of authenticity that is compatible with the drama such a genre makes possible. She skilfully exploits the 'double agent' status that literary critics accord it – between history and literature – to deliver a literary gem with a strong sense of historical realism.

6 Postcolonial and Postmodern Identities

Bethwell Ogot, Carlos Eire, Robert A. Rosenstone, Wang Gungwu

The most recent group of autobiographies, published in this century, share two essential qualities. First, they are all written by professional historians, teachers at prestigious African, Asian and North American universities. Second, they belong unequivocally to postcolonial and postmodern trends in featuring identity issues at their core. The result is Bethwell A. Ogot's dense, vindictive African memoir, Carlos Eire's delightful autobiography of childhood in an idealised pre-Castro Cuba, Wang Gungwu's multi-ethnic remembrance of postcolonial South Asia, and Robert A. Rosenstone's imaginative immigration story. All of them touch on

---

[105] Lerner, *Fireweed*, 371.

current and crucial issues such as the weight of the colonial tradition in academic circles, the influence of communism as a Western ideology projected onto previously colonised territories, the creation phase of new postcolonial identities, and the cultural transplantation that immigration entails.

For these authors, autobiography appears to be a solid platform for transmitting identity realities that require less conventional genres than the strictly academic. By practising autobiography, these historians seem to have deliberately broken the rules of the game entailing conventional – and in some sense arbitrary – boundaries that keep historians and other scholars from sharing things they know, or think they know. This is especially significant in Eire's denunciation of the Castro regime, Ogot's painful accusation against hegemonic Western historiography in African history, Gungwu's intelligent defence of inter-ethnic, interreligious and meta-national coexistence in Southeast Asia, and Rosenstone's deep reflections on the functioning of personal and collective memory.

Moreover, each of these authors practises a particular subgenre: academic autobiography in Ogot's case, childhood autobiography in Eire's, family autobiography in Rosenstone's and conventional autobiography in Gungwu's. These diverse literary modes allow each of them to explore the themes they are most interested according to the 'modes of emplotment' proposed by Northrop Frye (*Anatomy of Criticism*) and Hayden White (*Metahistory*) that best correspond to their moods and historiographic tendencies: Ogot's tragedy, Eire's satire, Rosenstone's comedy and Gungwu's novel.

These different modes are also reflected in the diversity of their mastery of rhetoric and narrative. Eire and Rosenstone are able to write with the same techniques, procedures and results of the best fiction writers, while Ogot and Gungwu use heavy, sometimes clumsy or dense, prose. The former are better able to spin a coherent discourse to tell a life story, while the latter take cover in academic discourse to legitimise their writing. But they all reflect a postcolonial and postmodern sensibility that makes them amenable to joint analysis, and they constitute the latest generation of autobiographical historians to appear so far.

Bethwell A. Ogot's Resentful Autobiography (2003)

> *The work involved analysing the encounter between*
> *an individual's life, my life,*
> *and the grand narratives of Kenyan and African*
> *colonial and neo-colonial societies.*[106]

---

[106] Bethwell Ogot, *My Footprints on the Sands of Time* (Kisumu: Anyange Press, 2011), Prolegomenon.

Bethwell Allan Ogot's autobiography, published in 2003, focuses on his intellectual and historiographical journey. It has the added value of enlightening us on the academic environment of an African country, Kenya, of which we have few other testimonies. Its prose is dense, the plot convoluted and many of the details he recounts are seemingly inconsequential, especially when he rattles off a memorandum of his publications or conferences in the manner of a curriculum vitae. But its very thickness consolidates *My Footprints* as a major historical source for African historiography in the second half of the twentieth century.

Ogot was born in Gem, in the Siaya County of Kenya, in 1929. He studied at his local school in Ambira, the prestigious Maseno School, Makerere University College, the University of St. Andrews (Scotland), and the School of Oriental and African Studies (SOAS), University of London. He rose to prominence as a student leader while studying in London, participating in the Lancaster House Kenyan independence negotiations in 1960. There he became a close friend of Jaramogi Oginga Odinga, one of the most important politicians in Kenya's independence negotiations. He also worked alongside the activist Tom Mboya in 1969, and witnessed his dramatic assassination, which he recounts in one of the book's most harrowing passages.[107]

He was the president of the International Scientific Committee for the preparation of UNESCO's *General History of Africa*, editing the fifth volume and the *History of Humanity*. His autobiography focuses especially on his years as director of the International Louis Leakey Memorial Institute for African Pre-History (TILLMIAP), a section of the National Museums of Kenya (NMK). He was Chancellor of Moi University until 2013. He stays as Professor Emeritus at Maseno University.

His various roles as scholar, university governor, administrator and politician mean that his autobiography moves between intellectual, academic, political and ideological content. This mixture imbues the account with a rather vengeful, axe-grinding air, making of it a platform to justify his political and academic positions, and falling into victimhood when delineating discrimination in favour of Western historians who specialise in African history. The chosen cover photo, a very serious and circumspect-looking Ogot, seems to epitomise a history of setbacks. There are terrible life trajectories among historians, especially those who suffered Nazi persecution and experienced the Holocaust, but I know of no other autobiography with such a painful sense of suffering and revanchism. This is explained by his colonial – and postcolonial – context. As Ogot himself recounts in the Introduction, The work [of autobiography] involved analyzing the

---

[107] Ogot, *Footprints*, 226–228.

encounter between an individual's life, my life, and the grand narratives of Kenyan and African colonial and neo-colonial societies. [. . .] This then is the life story of an African scholar who has been profoundly shaped by his experiences and who seeks to understand both the world and himself through this process of interaction.[108]

From the first chapter, devoted to the description of his native region (Alara), the instability of the political context in which Ogot spent his childhood emerges. Proof of the westernisation of the area is that he never remembered seeing his father without a tie. He takes an ambivalent an approach to European colonisation in Africa. While there were some misdeeds, he also testifies to some obvious benefits, especially thanks to Christianisation:

> The critical role of African catechists and evangelists has rarely been fully appreciated, but as we have shown in the case of Alara, they were instrumental in establishing schools and churches (donating and providing building materials and labour), translating the scriptures, interpreting the Christian message, and conveying it to others.[109]

The autobiography is extremely detailed. In the style of Annie Kriegel's *C'est que j'ai cru comprendre* or Erich Hobsbawm's *Interesting Times*, it intersperses many documentary sources, such as letters or reports, quoted verbatim. It is therefore unlikely to appeal to many readers, except those of us who are interested in the specific genre of historians' autobiographies. Like the historians in the eastern modernisation section (Fukuzawa, Gu, Chaudhuri and Hussein), he showed from the beginning a great interest in analysing the original sources of African history with respect but matched by a radical critical spirit: 'My main preoccupation at SOAS for the next one year was the exploration and examination of the techniques of studying history in preliterate societies in Africa and in other parts of the world with a view to evolving my own methodology.'[110]

His training in Europe and contacts with European historians, especially Jan Vansina, earned him, even as late as 1961, criticism in his own country as a 'black European'.[111] However, he was the first casualty of the African academy's tendency to value Western criticism more highly than African criticism. He found that when he published his work in English in a Western journal, his ideas spread enormously, and his reputation grew in Africa itself. He attributed this to the fact that 'our people were yet to be decolonized since we still needed a foreign white man to convince us of the quality of our own words'.[112]

The autobiography becomes difficult to digest in the second part, where he details some of the events in which he has felt aggrieved. In the very long

---

[108] Ogot, *Footprints*, i.   [109] Ogot, *Footprints*, 10.   [110] Ogot, *Footprints*, 103.
[111] Ogot, *Footprints*, 114.   [112] Ogot, *Footprints*, 216.

passage defending his performance as director of the National Museum of Kenya, he records fears that there existed 'a conspiracy at establishing global intellectual hegemony of the West'.[113] Finally, he concluded,

> I learnt one important lesson from my experience in TILLMIAP, and that was that African governments must finance their own research institutions and programmes if they wish to achieve meaningful development. No research and development programmes based on donor funding alone, however substantial, can ever succeed anywhere, least of all in Africa.[114]

Out of this was born an ongoing struggle to enable Africa to govern its own cultural and academic institutions, and thus to seek the financial means to carry them out autonomously.

Ogot's autobiography shows that historians' memoirs, like those of any other academic, lose interest the more historical-historiographical they become, and the less *literary*. Autobiography is a particular genre that follows specific rules, the most important of which is the 'pact' between author and reader. As defined by Philippe Lejeune (*Le pacte autobiographique*, 2005), this pact involves the implicit understanding that the autobiographer functions as an author using their memory rather than as a historian analysing external primary sources to recount their own life. Retrospection is therefore strictly linked to introspection. The more 'literary' the historian-autobiographer becomes, the more they succeed in responding to the specific nature of the genre and are thus able to gain a more general audience. If they conceive of their autobiography as a strictly academic and historiographical artefact, as Ogot does, they reduce their audience to specialists in his discipline. The opposite is true of Carlos Eire's autobiography, our next case study.

Carlos Eire's Autobiography of Childhood (2003)

Occasionally, some things surface in dreams.[115]

Many of the readers of this Element will remember Elián's story. In 1999, Elián González, aged seven, left Cuba on a small boat with his mother and twelve other Cubans. On their way to the United States, the boat sank and Elián lost his mother. Once in the United States, he found himself in the midst of a political and media storm, in its own way perhaps even more virulent than the sea tempest that had killed his mother. Cuban American relatives took him to their home in Miami, but his father, who had stayed in Cuba, demanded his return to the island. The boy was sent back and re-entered Cuba to patriotic exaltation, hailed as a national hero, and declaring that he considered Castro 'not only a friend but a father'.

---

[113] Ogot, *Footprints*, 369.   [114] Ogot, *Footprints*, 371.
[115] Eire, *Waiting for Snow in Havana: Confessions of a Cuban Boy* (New York: Free Press, 2003), 107.

Located 2218 kilometres from the scene, a peaceful professor of early-modern history at Yale University fell into a state of rampant indignation – a kind of 'wrath of the meek'. The affair brought painful memories to the 14,000 Cuban boys who had arrived in America at the beginning of the 1960s without their parents in the so-called 'Operation Peter Pan' to save them from Castro's regime. The parents were supposed to be reunited with their children soon but Castro, aware of the CIA-sponsored operation, did not let them leave. Many of these children never saw their parents again – or never saw one of them, as in the case of Eire. Moved by Elián's story, Eire began writing his memories of childhood in pre-revolutionary Cuba compulsively during over a period of months, working at night from 10 p.m. to 3 a.m. The author's father, who died in 1976, never left Cuba. As he acknowledged some years after the publication of his memoir, the Elián González affair inspired him to write because:

> The sheer hypocrisy behind Castro's claim that every child should be with his or her parent [this was Castro's argument to claim for Elián's return to Cuba] was what angered me the most and brought up so many memories. It was like a volcanic eruption. One day I started writing and I couldn't stop.[116]

Carlos Eire was born in Havana in November 1950 and entered the United States in 1962 without his parents, who remained on the island. When he landed in the United States, he found himself, aged eleven, in a refugee camp for Cuban children at the edge of the Florida Everglades. After living in a series of foster homes in Florida and Illinois, he was reunited with his mother in Chicago in 1965, though he never saw his father again. He received his PhD from Yale in 1979, taught at St. John's University in Minnesota and the University of Virginia, and was a member of the Institute for Advanced Study in Princeton for two years. He finally joined the Yale faculty in 1996.

Waiting for Snow in Havana repeats the classic 'lost paradise' story of some childhood autobiographies. In vivid prose, it narrates Cuba's tragic shift when a 'cigar-smoking guerrilla' named Fidel Castro drove President Batista from the country on 1 January 1959. As Eire describes that day, the music in the streets suddenly started sounding like gunfire. Only 'the lizards remained oblivious to the news that day, as always'.[117] Christmas was made illegal, political dissent led to imprisonment and too many of Eire's friends were leaving Cuba for the United States. Written with the urgency of a confession, *Waiting for Snow in Havana* is an eulogy for a native land and a loving testament to the collective spirit of Cubans everywhere.

---

[116] Eire, *Waiting*, 395, paperback edition.   [117] Eire, *Waiting*, 3.

Following the specific logic and functioning of childhood autobiography, Eire enjoyed hearing (and then retelling) stories from his parents and relatives in his early years. He is especially expressive when narrating the 'firsts' of his childhood: the first time he got drunk, his first confession, and the first time he fell in love. Then, the sudden 'great event', Castro revolution, changed Cuba: 'The world changed while I slept, and much to my surprise, no one had consulted me. That's how it would always be from that day forward.'[118] By opening his memoir with those words, he foregrounds a historical event as the governing force for the narrative. While he uses various imaginative devices to describe his early years, such as metaphors, dreams and the introduction of invented characters, the narration becomes more realistic when describing his experiences after Castro revolution. The sharp contrast between the comic tone of the first part and the serious episodes of the second makes the story deeply tragic: the drama of a life broken with a lost paradise – his Cuban childhood – abruptly interrupted by the Castro revolution. Eire's vector of continuity is his idealised early years and his Cuban identity, while his vector of rupture is marked by Castro revolution and exile to the United States.

Though humorous in recounting his childhood, Eire judges Castro severely in the text. This tragic-comic strategy allows him to imbue reality with imagination without really telling lies – one of the terrible evils he, as a child, always tried to avoid because it could send him to the hell. The only acceptable criteria for childhood autobiographies are not historical accuracy but the typical internal and symbolic truth of the children. As he describes Cuban society under Castro, Eire presents a symbolic, rather than a literal, reality. The boy's vision stamps his mark especially because of his radical and apocalyptic sense of justice.

Waiting for Snow in Havana is an important reflection on two key concepts of historical postmodernism: the relationship between history and fiction, and the mediation of language. The prominence of these two concepts is connected not only to Eire and other postmodern autobiographers' historical training and epistemic options, but also to the specific characteristics of the genre of childhood autobiography. To begin with, he admits enjoying the writing of 'his first book without footnotes' and using of all the rhetorical options of autobiography.[119] Thus, he is not writing as a historian who takes advantage of his professional expertise to write his own story. Rather, he writes autobiographically, trusting memory and forgetting everything he had ever written before, as his wife advised him to do at the beginning of this literary project. He reveals his literary intentions from the beginning: 'This is not a work of fiction. But the author would like it to

---

[118] Eire, *Waiting*, 1.   [119] Eire, *Waiting*, 388.

be. We improve when we become fiction, each and every one of us, and when the past becomes a novel our memories are sharpened.'[120]

In this multiple dimension of Eire's memoir – history, memory, tradition, imagination – the author eventually feels obliged to support his claims, perhaps unable to radically forget his historical training as he tells the story of a child's growing awareness of the world around him. In the end, he shows that the writing of history is compatible with the honest use of memory and imagination, a king of 'magic realism' worthy of his counterparts in Latin American literature. His autobiography deals with the universal experiences of loss and separation, the joys, misunderstandings, sufferings and cruelties of childhood, and the good and evil consequences of human behaviour – which can be devastating when coming from politicians and revolutionaries.

Robert A. Rosenstone's Postmodern Autobiography (2005)

> *The reality of the past*
> *does not lie in an assemblage of data*
> *but in a field of stories.*[121]

Robert A. Rosenstone, a prominent specialist in history and film, makes of autobiography an academic artefact in itself. With his two familial and personal memories (*The Man Who Swam into History* in 2005 and *Adventures of a Postmodern Historian* in 2016), he proposes a better understanding of the past, his past and his historical discipline through a reflection on his own life.

Rosenstone was born in Montreal (Canada) in 1936. His parents were Jewish immigrants from Latvia and Romania respectively. He studied history at the University of California, Los Angeles, taught at the California Institute of Technology for most of his scholarly life, and he peacefully retired with his wife Nahid. He has published books which have challenged established disciplinary rules, and has always considered autobiographical reflection and practice to be part of his historical operation rather than 'in spite of' or 'apart' or 'different from' it.[122] This makes his autobiographical accounts real intellectual artefacts and experimental historical literature. He conceived his autobiographical essays as ways to connect personal experiences and family with academic interests:

> It never occurred to me that my [academic] choices might also connect to my heritage. That if you are born into an immigrant family with parents from two

---

[120] Eire, *Waiting*, 'Preámbulo'.
[121] Robert A. Rosenstone, *The Man Who Swam into History: The (Mostly) True Story of My Jewish Family* (Austin: University of Texas Press, 2005), xv.
[122] Jaume Aurell, 'Autobiography as Unconventional History: Constructing the Author', *Rethinking History* 10 (2006): 433–449.

cultures as different and conflicting in values as those of Latvia and Romania (the German and the Latin), a family in which racketeers and Communists and extramarital affairs were unremarkable, you might have a tendency to take an interest in characters torn between the values and beliefs of different worlds.[123]

Rosenstone's postmodern treatment of this material provides readers with a multi-layered and multi-voiced narrative of the Jewish diaspora. The literary structure of his two autobiographies resembles a collage or a mosaic more than a conventional linear narrative. In his *The Man Who Swam into History*, to increase this multi-perspective approach, he appropriates the voices of his grandmother Sarah, his grandfather Chaim Baer and his mother, Hannah, offering a hypothesis of these characters' thoughts regarding the world surrounding them. He also presents several versions of the founding heroic event of his family story, especially his grandfather's dramatic escape from Russia: 'My grandfather had swum the roaring and dangerous Prut River to get to Romania and escape the military draft in Russia. Only later did I learn almost every grandfather of every Jewish Romanian claimed the same athletic feat.'[124]

He reproduces family gossip, scandals, affairs – and his father and uncle Moishe's mob connections – from the perspective of a character called Rabin, himself. As in Eire's book, but through familial memoir rather than childhood autobiography, Rosenstone provides a hilarious, ironic, sometimes irreverent narration which seems to lessen the drama of the content of his story.

The literary, creative and imaginative character of Rosenstone's family memoir is linked to his inclination to deal, as a historian, with non-conventional subjects. The jargonistic language of history-as-science must be transformed into a narrative, discursive and comprehensible language. Rosenstone has confessed that his flirting with postmodernism was not the outcome of his prior knowledge of its theoretical postulates but rather of his awareness of the limitations of traditional historical narrative, which did not allow him to express to the full the experiences of his characters in the past. He seems to echo Edmund Carr's statement that 'Gerald Brenan once told me that he despaired of finding "truth" with the method of professional historians and that it could only be grasped by the unfettered imaginations in novels'.[125] Rosenstone came to appreciate the way postmodern theorists exposed the limitations of 'truth' as postulated by traditional history, which no longer satisfied his wish to present the reader with a history that was truly alive.

Rosenstone's decision to subtitle his family memoir 'The (Mostly) True Story of My Jewish Family' is an expression of intellectual honesty rather than

---

[123] Rosenstone, *The Man*, xi–xii.   [124] Rosenstone, *The Man*, xi.
[125] Edmund Carr, *Times Literary Supplement*, 23–29 June 1989.

postmodern provocation. In some sense, this rhetorical strategy forms part of the genre's identity, as Philippe Lejeune clarifies in his seminal phrase 'autobiographical pact'. As he states,

> anyone who has done historical research knows that it takes more than access to documents to create a truthful or meaningful past. The reality of the past— national, familial, personal—does not lie in an assemblage of data but in a field of stories—a place where fact, truth, fiction, invention, forgetting, and myth are so entangled that they cannot be separated. Ultimately it is not the facts that make us what we are, but the stories we have been told and the stories we believe.[126]

In his second memoir, *Adventures of a Postmodern Historian*, Rosenstone shows that the strict rules agreed by the founders of the discipline since the mid nineteenth century is one way to recover the past, but not the only one. This autobiography is a historical-narrative experiment in which Rosenstone tries to give practical effect to those suppositions that he himself has sought to incorporate in his historical practice throughout his career. He again employs three narrative voices: the properly retrospective-introspective one, as seen in the 'first person' form conventionally used by ego-historical historians; the historiographic one used by interventional-autobiographical historians, who in recent decades have used autobiography as a platform for theoretical reflection on the foundations of their discipline; and, finally, the fictional one used by some postmodern autobiographical historians, in which imaginary characters speak, personifying some specific circumstances remembered by the author, and appropriately framed to distinguish them from the two previous voices. The conjunction of these three voices is the most characteristic and remarkable feature of this autobiography, which apart from that is superbly well written, so that reading it has a notably magnetic effect on the reader – especially if they are a historian.

With the use of these three voices (the historical, the historiographic and the fictional), Rosenstone identifies himself with the Cubist style of Picasso's *Guernica*, one of the artistic works that has generated most fascination in him due to its double nature as sublime work of art and precise historical document – one 'which like any good work of history has come to replace the event it commemorates',[127] and which represents reality from different perspectives at the same time.

The Man Who Swam into History and *Adventures of a Postmodern Historian* are a works for those who still believe in the fascinating effect that telling stories

---

[126] Rosenstone, *The Man*, xv.
[127] Robert A. Rosenstone, *Adventures of a Postmodern Historian* (London: Bloomsbury Academic, 2016), 11.

produces, beyond an academic history that is in danger of losing its connection with society – and more crucially, with true referentiality to the reality of the past and present. Rosenstone's autobiographical accounts engage the complex relationship between history and fiction through his multi-voiced autobiographies, where he speaks simultaneously as a historian, historiographer and novelist.

Wang Gungwu's Postcolonial Autobiography (2018)

> *History was an open window to a wider canvas*
> *that covered everything that had a past*
> *that could be relevant to the present.*[128]

Wang Gungwu's autobiographies describe the postcolonial experiences of an Indonesian intellectual who taught at several universities in Southeast Asia like Hong Kong and Singapore, and subsequently in Australia. The two titles of his successive autobiographies well define his constant search for identity in the midst of a rapidly changing colonial and postcolonial world: from *Home is not Here* (2018) to *Home Is Where We Are* (2021). His continuous sense of change drives his narrative: 'I thought I should tell my children how different my world was before I left home so that they would understand what has changed for them as children and for us as their parents.'[129]

Wang was born in Surabaya and grew up in Ipoh, Malaysia. His parents were Chinese, and he specialised in the Chinese diaspora of Southeast Asia, to which he belonged. He studied at the University of Malaya, where he received a British education. He was a founder member of the University Socialist Club and its founding president in 1953, but he always stayed away from the activist struggle, with a scepticism similar to that of Chaudhuri in Bengal decades earlier. He received his PhD at SOAS, University of London (as did Ogot) for his thesis *The Structure of Power in North China during the Five Dynasties*. He was one of the founders of the Malaysian liberal political party Gerakan, but soon withdrew from the party's activities. He moved to the Australian National University in Canberra in 1968, to the University of Hong Kong in 1986, and to the National University of Singapore in 1995.

Wang acts as a postcolonial intellectual able to combine eastern and Western traditions without the dramatic tensions experienced by the 'colonised' historians of Section 4: 'I was using a platform that was dominated by both European historiography and elements of my Confucian self-improvement background.'[130] His father fostered in him a dual Sino-British upbringing, since he was both an

---

[128] Wang Gungwu, *Home Is Where We Are* (Singapore: National University of Singapore, 2021), 95.
[129] Wang Gungwu, *Home Is Not Here* (Singapore: National University of Singapore, 2018), 1.
[130] Gungwu, *Home Is Not Here*, 1.

enthusiast for Confucian thought and at the same time an admirer of English literature: 'He seems to have believed that the combination of Chinese and English literary culture would be a good start and fit me better for the modern world.'[131]

Just as Chaudhuri is an excellent testimony to the different cultures around India, Wang's is an account of the different Chinese cultures, from Dutch Java to British Malaya. He is therefore a multicultural personality, able to value the best of each culture rather than emphasising what separates them. He suffered the cultural logics inherent in the processes of colonisation, decolonisation and postcolonisation in the countries that make up the Chinese cultural area. He had to confront linguistic variety:

> I was influenced by the free verse popularized by modern English poets to try to capture some of the images of the mixed communities of Chinese, Malays, Indians and Eurasians that characterized Malayan society. We were unclear what language we should be using, so I used Malay and Chinese words in basically English sentence structures. We also thought we should not only use English speech patterns but also seek to capture a local voice or accent.[132]

When this colonial world collapsed after 1945, he did not take a radical anticolonial stance, but tried to recover the best of the South Asian and the West tradition:

> I was thus made aware that the English language connected us not only through our common anti-colonial experiences but also enabled us to share an admiration for English literature and ultimately the global literature in English. There were different dimensions of sensibility and such sharing had little to do with the political calls for Malayan literature.[133]

Wang sees himself as a protagonist in the creation of a new postcolonial Malayan identity. His strategy is to bring together a group of educated and passionate students to inspire future generations. The consolidation of an indigenous 'literary identity' seemed to him one of the most effective means of strengthening it. This led him to become more aware of anticolonial movements. However, he always favoured thoughtful analysis over revolutionary activism. So, he decided to stay out of political activities. Instead, he kept 'trying to understand what was happening'.[134] Yet history soon replaced literature as the main rhetorical strategy to reinforce Malayan identity. Why history?

> It was the combination of my personal inclinations and the experience of learning about the new Malayan environment that led me to choose history.

---

[131] Gungwu, *Home Is Not Here*, 14.   [132] Gungwu, *Home is Where We Are*, 20.
[133] Gungwu, *Home is Where We Are*, 55.   [134] Gungwu, *Home is Where We Are*, 93.

[. . .] [History] was an open window to a wider canvas that covered everything
that had a past that could be relevant to the present [. . .] Choosing to study
history also made me realize how much the past had influenced various parts
of my life.[135]

In his approach to the past, he tried to combine the Western 'linear chronology'
that sharpened the sense of cause and effect in the unfolding of events with
'cyclical perspectives' that he was familiar with from studying Chinese history.

Wang's autobiography is stimulating from a theoretical and practical perspective because its author does not tend to see nations, social classes, ethnici-
ties and civilisations in opposition, as was characteristic of the hegemonic
Marxist logics of his time, but rather in complementarity. However, his main
concern was problems associated with identity. His wife, Margaret Wang, offers
a clue to this at the end of his second autobiography (*Home Is Where We Are*).
When they were moving to Canberra, his last stop in academia, and packing
everything up, 'she looked around the house, contemplated what we were
bringing with us and turned to me saying, "home is where we are." I nodded,
I can settle for that'.[136] This new perspective changed the idea contained in the
title of the first autobiography (*Home Is Not Here*). Beyond the plurality of cities
and countries he has lived in, his universal awareness – and, above all, his being
in a university environment – has contributed to his never feeling 'out of place'
and provided us all with a good model of postcolonial coexistence.

Conclusions

Leo Tolstoy famously argued that 'the man who plays a part in a historical
drama never understands its true significance'.[137] The historians analysed in
this Element – living in all periods and belonging to all civilisations – have tried
to resist this reality in their attempt to project all their historical insight into
a retrospective view of their own lives. In my view, they have succeeded in their
enterprise, or at least they have succeeded in giving this author great enjoyment
in reading and re-reading their autobiographies. However, this brave venture
has had its price, since it has put historians on the front line of storytelling. They
have entered the world of artistic creation and poetic imagination, which has
challenged their own disciplinary training. But many of them already conceived
of their historical work as a creative process, which obviously made for more
engaging autobiographies: the more literary we find them, the more appealing
they are. This is the same quality that, as Hayden White argued, we find in the
historical classics:

---

[135] Gungwu, *Home is Where We Are*, 95.   [136] Gungwu, *Home is Where We Are*, 271.
[137] Quoted in Cohen, *Making*, 390.

Historiography adds something to a merely factual account of the past. This something added may be a pseudo-scientific explanation of why events happened as they did, but the recognised classics of Western historiography always add something else. And I think that it is 'literarity' which they add, for which the great modern novelists provide between models than the pseudo-scientists of society.[138]

In their historiographical practice, historians may take refuge behind the barricade of scholarly jargon or erudite footnotes. But when they practise autobiography, they lose the cover of academic formalisms. This combination of historicity and literariness is what makes the autobiographies of Gibbon, Adams, Steedman, Conway, Lerner, Eire and Rosenstone unique – some of their authors having had to overcome traumas caused by totalitarian regimes or racial and gender discrimination. This does not diminish the quality of the autobiographies of ancient and medieval historians, but the interest of these works lies rather in their ability to explore aspects of the past that we would not otherwise have known, such as the justification of the historian's vocation (Sima, Lucian), the motivations of the authoritarian leader (Caesar, King Peter) or the psychology of the crusader (Geoffrey). They function more as primary sources than as narrative artefacts of a specifically autobiographical category.

This leads us to reflect on two essential questions in relation to the practice of this autobiographical subgenre: their function as historical sources and the diversity of their literary-autobiographical styles.

Regarding the first of these, their character and function as sources centre above all on questions of intellectual history and, more specifically, of historiography. Of course, there are other sources for studying the historian's life, intellectual training, academic itinerary, historiographical relevance and the circumstances of the production of their historical works: the prefaces to their works, correspondence, diaries and interviews, among others. All of these are privileged sources that allow us to enter the intellectual universe surrounding the life of each historian. In addition, we historians familiarising ourselves with the first principles of source criticism quickly learn to distrust autobiographies as a genre full of bias and self-interest. Once we learn a bit more about narrative representation and self-fashioning, we have another reason to read autobiographies with a heightened degree of suspicion. All this is true, but I hope I have shown that there are nonetheless good reasons for reading historians' autobiographies, not as faithful accounts of their lives and work, but as stimuli for reflection. Historians' autobiographies add the nuance of moving through a narrative sequence that provides a global vision of their life, the actions,

---

[138] Hayden White, 'An Old Question Raised Again: Is Historiography Art or Science?' *Rethinking History* 4 (2000): 391–406, here 395.

choices, successes, failures, obsessions, emotions, attachments, spirituality, illnesses, family, tragedies, goals and character of which are better understood because they can be related to each other.

The second question concerns the different autobiographical styles used by historians turned autobiographers. I have distinguished three autobiographical styles among the historian-autobiographers analysed in this Element: biographical, poetic and interventional. I based this subgenre classification on thematic categories and stylistic features beyond their chronology. The categories are not rigid, of course, and some writers fit into two or three styles, as is the case with Adams and Steedman.

The most common style, used by Caesar, Geoffrey, King Peter, Ibn Khaldun, Gibbon, Fukuzawa, Hussein, Chaudhuri, Conway, Lerner and Gungwu, is the biographical. These authors construct their life-writing stories in a descriptive mode, while trying to understand the life that is theirs. They tend to explain the events they have experienced rather than engage with them in formal experimentation or with particular historiographical sophistication. Except in cases where they are interested in emphasising a particular aspect of their lives – such as Caesar's participation in battles or Geoffrey's in crusades – they usually proceed by recounting their entire lives from childhood to the moment they decide to write their memoirs. In doing so, they provide us with an integrated vision of their lives, in which the drama of the events unfolding in the imagination and historical memory of their authors are brought together.

Most of these *biographical* historians – I am particularly thinking of Gibbon, Adams, Chaudhuri, Conway, Lerner and Gungwu – design their autobiographies in the same way they articulate their historical texts: by foregrounding objectivity and establishing critical distance between the subject –the historian who narrates the story – and the object, their own life. They aspire to distance themselves from their own texts in order to gain credibility, theoretically opposed to the genre they are writing, which highlights a complete identification between author and text. Certainly, they have been trained in the belief that the boundaries of verisimilitude are clearer the more distant the historian is from the historical events represented. Yet when they function as autobiographers, they discover that this subject-object and author-narration separation is very difficult to maintain, since the content of their narrations is life itself. It is for this reason that authors such as Gibbon and Adams experience a certain contradiction of genre, since they function as historian-biographers who write an autobiography, leading to a certain heaviness in some of their passages.

The second autobiographical style, practised by Lucian, Steedman, Lerner, Eire and Rosenstone, is the poetic. They understand themselves to be actors in history, so they create themselves in a narrative act. In a sense, it is an act of *re*-creation – they are the only group among historian-autobiographers who write ironically about themselves. This is not because they consider themselves *less* as historians than the others, but because of their poetic – *and* postmodern, in the case of Rosenstone, Steedman and Eire – conception of history. They believe that experimental forms of writing history – autobiography among them – are not alien to the existing conventions. Rather, they think these are simply other forms of representing the past, different but complementary to more traditional historical genres such as biography or monograph. Thus, their autobiographical intention is performative and aesthetic rather than just descriptive or memoiristic. Their autobiographies are highly performative, where saying something involves doing something. The function is not only heuristic, descriptive or memoiristic, because these authors want to create a personal awareness of something and contribute to its collective consciousness: Lucian reaffirming his intellectual choice through a dream, Steedman expanding class consciousness through her childhood memories, Lerner contributing to women's emancipation by narrating her dramatic life struggle, Eire denouncing a dictatorship by recalling his childhood, and Rosenstone revealing the richness of multi-ethnic and multicultural environments through his family memoir. In addition, the autobiographies constructed by these poetic and experimental historians are more literary and imaginative: they also reveal more about the epistemological nature of life-writing and of authorial intervention itself.

For poetic-autobiographical authors such as Steedman, Conway, Lerner, Eire and Rosenstone, the practice of autobiography became a liberation. In fact, Rosenstone admitted to this author that, with his autobiographies, he was trying to get rid of the straitjacket of academic formalisms that constrict historians' discourse. Carlos Eire puts it differently when he admits enjoying writing his autobiography as 'his first book without footnotes'.[139]

The third autobiographical mode, which some twentieth-century French historians who became autobiographers would call *ego-histoire*, is the interventional style as practised by Sima, Vico, Jiegang and Ogot. These authors are, above all, concerned with recounting the part of their lives related to scholarship, with the intention of *intervening* in the historiographical debates of their time. They privilege the professional over the personal in their autobiographical writing. Intellectual and academic life occupies centre stage in these self-representations, and other issues – particularly personal information – are relegated to second place, if mentioned at all. The authors' aim is to highlight their academic itineraries, and they stress key points in their professional careers: a dramatic moment of personal and intellectual crisis in the case of

---

[139] Eire, *Waiting for Snow in Havana*, 388.

Sima, the intellectual itinerary that has contributed to such an influential work as Vico's, the justification of a critical approach to a received tradition in the case of Jiegang, and academic self-justification in the case of Ogot. They see autobiography more as a duty of justification than as an opportunity to enjoy the freedoms of imaginative prose.

The spectrum of these three styles moves from Ogot's detailed interventional narrative to Rosenstone's rhetorical freedom. The former reads as a historical artefact of a recent past, the latter as an imaginative reconstruction of lived experience. We now better understand some historians' reluctance to turn to autobiography; and why, when they do decide to do it, they take care not to be 'too autobiographical'. As the British social historian Geoff Eley has acknowledged, 'in telling my own story I'm aware of taking a risk' – and consequently, 'it was in the interests of not becoming too autobiographical that I decided to leave much of the detail out'.[140] Perhaps not unrelated to this reluctance is the fact that four of the autobiographers presented in this study (Hussein, Caesar, Vico and Adams) have used the rhetorical effect of writing their memoirs in the third person.

But beyond historians' identification or disaffection with the practice of the genre, and the three autobiographical styles developed, all of these autobiographies by historians show their full practical and vindicatory potential, especially in the sections on colonised and postcolonised historians, as well as on women historians. These authors have tried to improve specific aspects of society through the practice of autobiography, by for example moderating the extremes in the anti-colonisation period (Fukuzawa, Taha Hussein, Gu, Chaudhuri), advocating for women (Steedman, Conway, Lerner), resisting dictatorship (Eire) and harmonising different cultures in one common experience (Wang, Rosenstone). The treatment of particularly sensitive topics for today's audiences, such as Adams' liberal view of existence, Steedman's class consciousness, Lerner's resistance to trauma, Conway's struggle for women's liberation or Eire's resistance to authoritarianism, has made some of them real bestsellers. This connection with large audiences is something that, admittedly, would have been impossible to achieve had these stories been presented in the more traditional genres of history such as monographs, biographies or academic papers.

This would not have been possible without the ability of some authors to *use* autobiography as an unconventional narrative experiment, even innovating in the creation of new genres, as is the case with Steedman, Eire and Rosenstone. They have abandoned the idea of autobiography as just *another* academic

---

[140] Geoff Eley, *A Crooked Line: From Cultural History to the History of Society* (Ann Arbor: University of Michigan Press, 2005), ix.

genre – different from history – as they have instrumentalised it to convey historical realities they could not otherwise express. These historians have assumed the challenge of the continued renewal of genre boundaries, experimenting with new literary forms that have located them at the frontiers of disciplinary innovation.

This experimentation with the autobiographical genre has even allowed some to become historians through autobiography when the opposite is more usual – historians who at some point in their careers decide to practise autobiography. Throughout these pages, we have seen three very special and particularly expressive cases, given the prodigious quality of the historical works that these historians published together with their autobiographies: Adams, Chaudhuri and Lerner. The latter repeats many times in her autobiography that her dream was to be a 'writer', but that she was finally able to become one through the practice of history and autobiography together.

These historians turned autobiographers are convinced, as one of them, Conway, once put it, that the 'magical opportunity of entering another life is what really sets us thinking about our own'.[141] Their autobiographies thus function as mirrors in which colleagues see themselves and ask questions about their own itineraries, choices and decisions. They make historians pose questions about the relationship between historical contexts and the historiographical changes that they have experienced themselves. They allow historians to better understand, by analogy, the contexts of the past and the transformations undergone by those contexts. They make historians think about the past and the present of the discipline, how and why they have come to the present disciplinary terms. They contain an implicit moral value that projects the discipline towards the future, since these autobiographies provide powerful stimuli for reflection on the political engagements and theoretical challenges of history, both as written and as experienced. In the end, this is the historiographical value of historians' autobiographies.

Reading the autobiographies of historians is so exemplary – especially for their fellow historians – that one leads to another. The historians turned autobiographers, from forerunners such as Sima Qian to more recent figures such as Wang Gungwu, are governed by that sublime aspiration to which all historians should feel attracted: not only to describe the *historical* truth, but the truth itself. As the Australian historian-autobiographer Sheila Fitzpatrick claimed, '[my] private sense of achievement was more exalted: I felt that, after all the agonising, what I had arrived at was *true*, even *the truth*. That was a nice feeling for a congenital relativist'.[142]

---

[141] Jill K. Conway, *When Memory Speaks: Exploring the Art of Autobiography* (New York: Vintage Books, 1999), 18.

[142] Sheila Fitzpatrick, 'Can You Write a History of Yourself? Thoughts of a Historian Turned Memoirist', *Griffith Review* 33 (2011): 1–7, here 7. Emphasis in the original.

The case studies presented here provide sufficient clues to understand historians' autobiographies and assign them the importance they deserve. Historians seem to have found a new genre that allows them to delve into the interactions between themselves, their historical research and the context in which they have lived. These texts function ambivalently as autobiographical testimony, life-writing, primary sources of intellectual history, and historiographical exploration. They therefore have literary and historical value, and both a theoretical and a practical dimension. They improve our knowledge of the past – and crucially, of the human condition. They help to define, analyse, understand and promote history and some of its subfields, such as gender history, social history and the history of historiography.

In the end, I would like to argue that historians' autobiographies may no longer be considered an unconventional historiographical genre. They can be used instead as a conventional historical and historiographical artefact as well as a source of intellectual history, with all the precautions that must be taken with texts of this nature. Their practice can even improve the way we access, understand, interpret and express the past. As a result of the approach I have proposed here, I suggest that the study and reading of these autobiographies should form part of the core curriculum of any historian's training.

Cambridge Elements ≡

Historical Theory and Practice

Daniel Woolf

Queen's University, Ontario

Daniel Woolf is Professor of History at Queen's University, where he served for ten years as Principal and Vice-Chancellor, and has held academic appointments at a number of Canadian universities. He is the author or editor of several books and articles on the history of historical thought and writing, and on early modern British intellectual history, including most recently *A Concise History of History* (CUP 2019). He is a Fellow of the Royal Historical Society, the Royal Society of Canada, and the Society of Antiquaries of London. He is married with 3 adult children.

About the Series

Cambridge Elements in Historical Theory and Practice is a series intended for a wide range of students, scholars, and others whose interests involve engagement with the past. Topics include the theoretical, ethical, and philosophical issues involved in doing history, the interconnections between history and other disciplines and questions of method, and the application of historical knowledge to contemporary global and social issues such as climate change, reconciliation and justice, heritage, and identity politics.

Cambridge Elements ⚌

Historical Theory and Practice

Elements in the Series

A full series listing is available at: www.cambridge.org/EHTP

Printed in the United States
by Baker & Taylor Publisher Services